BUSES

ALONG THE SOUTH WEST COAST PATH from MINEHEAD to POOLE HARBOUR via LAND'S END

A HISTORY OF THE PAST & A GUIDE TO THE MODERN DAY

ANDREW BARTLETT

PEN & SWORD
TRANSPORT

AN IMPRINT OF PEN & SWORD BOOKS LTD.
YORKSHIRE – PHILADELPHIA

First published in Great Britain in 2020 by
Pen and Sword Transport
An imprint of
Pen & Sword Books Ltd
Yorkshire - Philadelphia

Copyright © Andrew Bartlett, 2020

ISBN 9781526755421

A CIP catalogue record for this book is available from the British Library.

Book design: Paul Wilkinson
Printed and bound in India by Replika Press Pvt. Ltd.

Pen & Sword Books Ltd incorporates the Imprints of Pen & Sword Books Archaeology, Atlas, Aviation, Battleground, Discovery, Family History, History, Maritime, Military, Naval, Politics, Railways, Select, Transport, True Crime, Fiction, Frontline Books, Leo Cooper, Praetorian Press, Seaforth Publishing, Wharncliffe and White Owl.

For a complete list of Pen & Sword titles please contact
PEN & SWORD BOOKS LIMITED
47 Church Street, Barnsley, South Yorkshire, S70 2AS, England
E-mail: enquiries@pen-and-sword.co.uk
Website: www.pen-and-sword.co.uk
or
PEN AND SWORD BOOKS
1950 Lawrence Rd, Havertown, PA 19083, USA
E-mail: Uspen-and-sword@casematepublishers.com
Website: www.penandswordbooks.com

Maps kindly supplied by mapmoose.com contain OS data © Crown copyright and database right 2011

Contents

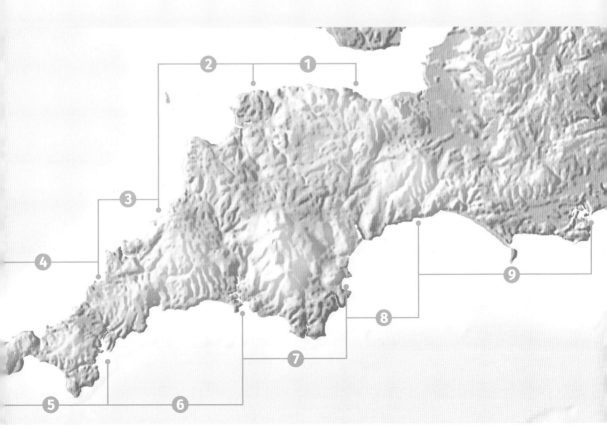

Setting the Scene

THE SOUTH WEST COAST PATH is, at the time of writing, the longest footpath and National Trail in England, covering some 630 miles (1,014 kilometres). It starts in Somerset, on Quay Street in Minehead, and traverses the entire north Devon and Cornwall coasts until it reaches Land's End. It then heads east, back through Cornwall and Devon and into Dorset, until it reaches journey's end at South Haven Point, a stone's throw from Poole Harbour. The path was created in several stages and was finally completed in 1978. The glorious scenery encountered along the route has led to the Path regularly appearing in lists of the world's best walks. It has become commonplace to see signposts such as the one illustrated here; the acorn is the symbol of a National Trail, and the counties of Somerset, Devon, Cornwall and Dorset are particularly fortunate to have such a truly spectacular trail on their own doorsteps.

But how have I made this connection between the Path and public transport? Well, having recently completed a study of Western National buses in Devon and Cornwall, I found I was left with a considerable number of other photographs, the best of which I felt merited inclusion in another volume. As a means of presenting an album of buses in the south-west, why not use the Path as the common denominator? And no need to limit it to current operators or Western National either. Whilst it, along with sister company

Southern National, Devon General and Hants & Dorset/Wilts & Dorset may have held dominion over large swathes of these coastal regions across the years, they were by no means the only ones.

Another consideration occurred to me. I cannot be the only one who, when visiting somewhere different, is interested to know what tourist attractions the area has to offer; that way I have spent many hours of discovery that might otherwise have passed me by. During the last forty years, through both holidays and work in the south-west of England, I have probably visited most seaside towns and villages along the route of the Path, and wandered along a good many sections of it too – though rarely for more than a mile at a time. It is generally reckoned that to undertake all 630 miles in one fell swoop would take around eight weeks, and perhaps only the very committed do that. But it is noteworthy that the *Complete Guide to The South West Coast Path*, published by the Association that oversees all aspects of the Path, whilst giving readers detailed information on the route and what they might encounter on each section, also helpfully sets out details of public transport for those who would prefer the bus/walk approach. And that set me thinking...

So I ask my reader to imagine him or herself at the front of an imaginary tour bus, stopping at many of the key points along the Path where they may observe the wide variety of vehicles that have served them over the past ten decades. I have included brief notes on the way in which the Path connects these places and the availability of modern-day bus services between them, as well as things that might be of interest to them along its route. Should any further encouragement be needed to plan a visit to the area, there are scenic views of some of the best locations as well.

I can strongly recommend the guide published by the South West Coast Path Association referred to above, which is updated every couple of years; the latest edition is for 2020/21. Its website – www.southwestcoastpath.org.uk – is also full of useful information.

The West Country Historic Omnibus and Transport Trust (www.busmuseum.org) is highly recommended for those wanting to know more about public transport in the south west.

Most of the photographs here are my own, but I am grateful to those who have let me include examples of their work; they are credited in the appropriate captions. Also some of the scenic photographs have been sourced from Adobe Stock picture library. I also want to thank my wife Debbie, who loves this part of the world as much as I do, Paul Wilkinson and Janet Brookes at Pen & Sword, Chris Aston, Alan Carter, Ray and Richard Prior for their help, and Paddy Poulton, for the happy days working with his team in St Austell.

Andrew Bartlett

Minehead to Ilfracombe: 40 Miles

On this section

The marker denoting the official start of the South West Coast Path was erected in 2001 and can be found on the seafront walk alongside Quay Street on the western side of Minehead. The port of Porlock Weir, reached after 9 miles, has a history stretching back well over 1,000 years and is popular with tourists. Some of its buildings date from the seventeenth century. Crossing the border into Devon, there are magnificent sea views to be had on the way to Lynmouth. Lynton, which stands on high cliffs directly above, is accessed either by the Path or by a cliff railway. Before reaching Combe Martin, the Great Hangman, at 1,043ft and with a cliff face of 800ft, is the highest sea cliff in England and the highest point on the entire Path. The final 5 miles to Ilfracombe are characterised by a series of headlands interspersed with bays, the largest of which is Watermouth Cove.

Things to see

Minehead is the terminus of the heritage West Somerset Railway, a 20-mile line which starts from Bishops Lydeard, 4 miles from Taunton. From Porlock to Lynton and Lynmouth and beyond, the route covers the northern part of the Exmoor National

The South West Coast Path marker at Minehead.

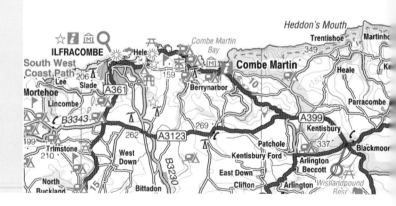

Park, and whether one is walking the Path or driving along the A39, there are magnificent views to be had. Lynmouth is where, in August 1952, exceptional storms caused the East and West Lyn rivers, which meet in the village, to flood catastrophically, with considerable loss of life. It is arguably most famous nowadays for the cliff railway that links it with Lynton, which at one time was the eastern terminus of the Lynton & Barnstaple narrow-gauge railway. This has been partially restored, and currently operates between Woody Bay and Killington Lane, although the plan is to eventually reinstate the original line in its entirety.

The route out of Lynton passes through the Valley of Rocks, where feral goats wander freely. Combe Martin is a small, popular seaside resort. This section of the Path ends in Ilfracombe, which has a small harbour, upon whose pier stands a Damien Hurst

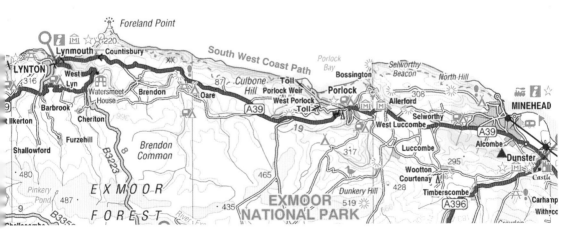

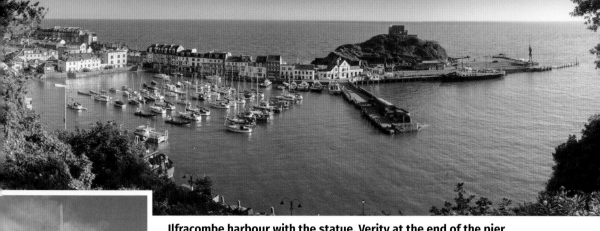

Ilfracombe harbour with the statue, Verity at the end of the pier.

statue, Verity. The town also boasts attractions such as a museum, aquarium, and theatre.

An outline of bus services past...

The history of bus services in the area in the 1920s is dominated by Colwills (Ilfracombe) Ltd and Hardy Central Garage, which traded as Hardy Colwills from April 1924. National took over in 1927. Southern National provided services between Ilfracombe and Combe Martin, and Lynton from 1929; Lynton was also linked to Barnstaple at this time. The route between Minehead and Lynton was in the hands of Porter, trading as Lorna Doone Coaches, until May 1930, when it was acquired by Western National. After forty years of peaceful coexistence, the Southern National name was lost in 1969 upon the foundation of the National Bus Company (NBC), but it was resurrected in 1983 as the government prepared for privatisation of the bus industry. A new company, North Devon (Red Bus), was formed at the same time, whose territory covered the North Devon coast from Lynmouth to Hartland, and south to Torrington and Tiverton. FirstGroup acquired both companies in 1999, putting Red Bus under Western National control, but quit the area in 2012. Stagecoach then became the dominant operator from Combe Martin westwards, with Filers Travel picking up several tendered routes. Southern National has received various fleetnames whilst under First jurisdiction, the latest being Buses of Somerset.

...and present

This section is not densely populated, and outside of the peak summer season, links between settlements along the path simply do not exist:

- AtWest, W. Ridler & Sons and First Buses of Somerset all input to service 10, which links Minehead with Porlock Weir (and return to Porlock).

• Quantock Heritage service 300 links Porlock and Lynmouth but only on summer weekdays.
• Lynmouth, Lynton and Combe Martin used to be connected by the 300, but no longer; there is no current service between these locations. The only alternative is to use Filers Travel services 309 to Barnstaple and 301 to Combe Martin, which calls at Ilfracombe en route.

A TRANSPORT-RELATED photo at the start of the Path is not possible, so instead we go eastwards for a couple of miles, to Butlin's Minehead resort in Warren Road, where the holiday camp was opened in 1962. The 300, or 'Exmoor Coastlink', was a joint operation between two FirstGroup companies, Southern National and Red Bus, and in 2000 ran daily during the summer months. Red Bus worked Barnstaple–Ilfracombe–Minehead, then Minehead–Lynmouth and return, and finally the reverse of its first journey. Its Southern National counterpart will be seen later, but this is Red Bus 4003 (K805 WTT), a Wright Handybus-bodied Dennis Dart, waiting to form the 16:15 departure for Barnstaple on 24 June.

SOMETIMES THE WEATHER on the Bristol Channel coast can be unpredictable. The forecast for Saturday, 20 September 2008, was for cloudy conditions, but the mist that had prevailed for most of the morning gave way to sombre cloud. This does not appear to have deterred the fair number of passengers aboard Quantock Motor Services YN55 RDV, a Scania N94UD/East Lancs OmniDekka new in October 2005, seen in The Avenue, Minehead when bound for Lynmouth. There it would meet up with the Filers Travel vehicle working the Ilfracombe to Lynmouth portion. At this time, the summer service still operated every day.

NINE MILES WEST of Minehead is the coastal village of Porlock Weir. Blue Motors provided the original service to Minehead, but competition arrived in 1928 in the shape of Mascot Safety Cars. Western National bought out the latter concern and their Minehead–Porlock Weir route became the 267, run jointly with Blue Motors until 1953. The principal operator now is a charitable organisation, Atwest (Accessible Transport West

Somerset), which was founded in 2005. Arriving in Porlock Weir on a mid-afternoon working on 21 May 2018, on what is now the 10, is route-branded Iveco WG63 FCN. W. Ridler & Son also provide two weekday services to and from Minehead Hospital and Tesco.

Lynton Church and Castle Hill.

I VISITED LYNTON in June 2019 and surveyed this scene from an almost identical position to the photographer here. Buses do not visit this part of the town now, but in the late 1920s (this postcard was sent to Sheffield in September 1929) there was sufficient room for the charabancs to line up and await passengers for their afternoon trips to Exmoor's Hunters Inn and Doone Valley. The scene is so obviously of a time long gone, yet in all other respects Castle Hill has not changed significantly in the past ninety years. It is just possible to close one's eyes and return to that bygone age and imagine the hustle and bustle as departure time approached.

FIRST BUSES IN Somerset still have a presence in Porlock Weir in 2019, also numbered 10, which provides a schooldays' service for the West Somerset College. Appearing half an hour after the Atwest vehicle and about to turn into the reversing area prior to depositing the last of its homeward-bound students, 68568 (BV57 MSU), is a BMC 1100 in time-honoured yellow school bus livery.

SOUTHERN NATIONAL INHERITED the 110 Barnstaple–Lynton service from National in 1929; it was renumbered 310 during NBC days and after the formation of North Devon (Red Bus) in 1983. The Cawlett group, which comprised North Devon and Southern National, was acquired by First in 1999, and county council contracts for underperforming routes were gradually abandoned. By 2008, the 310 was in the hands of TW Coaches, based in South Molton, whose Mercedes Vario O814 V1 TWC was pictured as it arrived in Lynton in September of that year, standing outside the famous Lynton and Lynmouth Cliff Railway.

In 2019, Lynton and Minehead are served by Quantock Heritage, but only twice a day, Mondays to Fridays, between 15 July and 6 September.

THIS IS THE Lynton and Lynmouth Cliff Railway in operation in a photo taken in July 2002. It was designed by George Marks as a water-powered funicular, and funded by publisher and philanthropist Sir George Newnes. It carried its first passengers on Easter Monday in 1890 and has been in almost continuous use ever since. Each car carries forty passengers; the line rises by 500ft from Lynmouth at a gradient of 58 per cent (1:1.7). It has now received listed monument status.

As the photo shows, both cars are fitted with water tanks that hold 700 gallons. Water is piped from the West Lyn River, over a mile away. When discharged from the lower car, the one at the top, now being the heavier, begins its descent. A brakeman rides on each car to ensure the speed is controlled.

THERE HAS BEEN a settlement at Ilfracombe since the Iron Age, though its importance as a holiday destination dates back to the early 1800s. Originally, public transport was very much the preserve of the Colwill family until National in 1927, and Southern National in 1929, took control. But this, the first of two photos in the town, takes us to June 2000, a year into the FirstGroup era. The last traces of Southern National in its former heartland in the north of Devon came with the jointly operated 300 Taunton–Barnstaple service. This vehicle, First Southern National Dennis Dart/Wright Handybus 806 (K328 KYC), was working the 300 in tandem with First Red Bus 4003, seen earlier in Minehead. 806 has arrived in Ilfracombe from Taunton; next will come an Ilfracombe–Lynmouth return, followed by the reverse of its first journey.

COLWILLS WAS FIRST to populate the principal Ilfracombe–
Barnstaple–Bideford–Westward Ho! corridor, which has been
variously numbered 1, 101, 301 and, in Red Bus days, 1 again.
Leyland Olympian/Alexander RL 1756 (L155 UNS) has just arrived
at the Ropery Road bus station from Westward Ho! on 24 June
2000. It had been transferred from Glasgow three months
earlier, but would move to Plymouth in May 2001 for Western
National's 82 service across Dartmoor. Ilfracombe depot, which
occupied part of the same site, opened in 1932, but was sold for
redevelopment in 2013; buses now use St James Place Gardens. In
2019, Stagecoach South West operate Ilfracombe–Westward Ho!
as the 21, and a trial in December 2018 led to the introduction of
the N21 night bus service between Ilfracombe and Bideford from
May 2019.

Ilfracombe to Boscastle: 100 Miles

Total so far: 140 Miles

On this section

Leaving Ilfracombe, the Path continues south-westerly past Lee Bay before arriving in Woolacombe. The beach, which stretches for 3 miles, has twice won 'Britain's Best Beach' awards in the 2010s, and is part of the North Devon Coast Area of Outstanding Natural Beauty. Next comes Mortehoe, which had a railway station jointly with Woolacombe on the Ilfracombe branch until its closure in 1970. Croyde and Braunton are passed before reaching Barnstaple. The River Taw, upon which the town stands, joins the River Torridge near Instow, which is passed en route to Bideford. Appledore and Westward Ho! stand on the Taw and Torridge estuary. Clovelly, pictured later in this chapter, comes next. The Path turns southwards after Hartland Point, crossing the border into Cornwall before arriving at the resort of Bude. It is a further 16 miles to Boscastle, via Widemouth Bay and Crackington Haven. This whole section of the Path since Clovelly has been characterised by high cliffs, and the terrain for walkers is described as severe in places.

Things to see

Surfing is a major sporting activity along this stretch of coastline, beginning at Woolacombe and continuing until Newquay. Braunton is important for its eponymous Burrows, the largest sand dune system in England. It also lays claim to being one of the largest villages in England, and the Path in this area utilises the former railway track that in years past played host to the Atlantic Coast

Woolacombe beach.

Bideford town and the Long Bridge spanning the River Torridge connecting the East and West of the town.

Express and now forms part of the Tarka Trail (based on the journey of Henry Williamson's fictional otter).

Barnstaple is the largest town in North Devon; its Pannier Market is well worth a visit. Bideford is a historic port mentioned in the Domesday Book and played a key role in maintaining Western and Southern National services during the Second World War, after the bombing of Plymouth had all but destroyed the Laira Bridge depot. The Riverside Works became the main overhaul works, a situation that carried on well into the 1950s.

Westward Ho! was named after the novel by Charles Kingsley, set in Bideford and published in 1855. The use of the exclamation mark in the name makes it unique in the British Isles.

An outline of bus services past...

The history of bus services in the area follows that in the previous chapter, where Hardy Colwills, National and Southern National were the major players. Bude was first reached in May 1922 and was the dividing line between Western National and North Devon (Red Bus) activities from 1983 onwards.

...and present

Following the route of the Path by bus between Ilfracombe and Boscastle in 2019 requires a certain amount of backtracking:

• Filers Travel service 31 links Ilfracombe and Woolacombe – return to Mullacott Cross
• Stagecoach South West services 21/21A link Mullacott Cross, Croyde, Barnstaple and Bideford. The 21 continues to Westward Ho! and the 21A to Appledore. Both Westward Ho!

and Appledore need to be visited separately, returning to Bideford each time
• Stagecoach South West service 319 links Bideford, Clovelly and Hartland, with the 219/319 continuing to Bude
• First Kernow service 95 links Bude and Boscastle

WITH THE WATERS of Morte Bay sparkling in the background, First Red Bus National 2802 (HTA 844N) begins the climb out of Woolacombe in June 2000. It began life with Western National in 1975 when it carried the fleet number 2813 but was renumbered by First in 1999; it was withdrawn in 2001 and has since entered preservation, carrying the NBC green livery it had when new. By 2000, the delightful resort of Woolacombe had a solitary link to Barnstaple (the 303) but three to Ilfracombe: the 31A was a more direct, and therefore slightly shorter, variant of the 31, while the 311 was a twice a day circular which, like the 31A, operated only in summer. The 31 and 303 still serve Woolacombe, but like many services that are insufficiently profitable to interest the likes of Stagecoach, they are now in the hands of Filers Travel.

REPRESENTATIVE OF WESTERN National's large fleet of Bristol RELLs, 2734 (STT 732H) passes through Braunton on its way to Barnstaple, Bideford and Westward Ho! on 3 September 1975. New in May 1970, it spent the next twelve years at Ilfracombe depot, and was one of eighteen of the type to pass to North Devon (Red Bus) in 1983, although it was withdrawn the following year.

WHEN NORTH DEVON (Red Bus) reorganised its services at the time of deregulation in 1986, Ilfracombe-based Filers Travel stepped in to restore certain links that had been broken. This move culminated in the complete reinstatement of the former 301 service between Ilfracombe and Westward Ho! and thus led to competition between the two companies. In 1994, Filers acquired J227 OKX, a 3-year-old Iveco Turbo City with Alexander RH H50/31F bodywork, which could often be found on the route. It was the only one of its kind in Great Britain, and had originally been used a demonstrator, Iveco hoping that it would gain them a foothold in the big bus market. It never did. I saw it in July 1997, loading for Bideford in Boutport Street, Barnstaple; behind it is North Devon (Red Bus) 'Atlantic Blue' Ford Transit 420 (C341 GJF).

THE OLDEST MEMBER of the North Devon (Red Bus) fleet upon its formation was this Roe-bodied Leyland Atlantean, 920 (920 GTA), new to Devon General in 1961 but which made its way to Barnstaple from Camborne in Cornwall during 1982. The new manager decided on Red Bus as a fleetname, but inherited a fleet decked out in NBC green. To overcome this minor difficulty, vehicles carried larger than normal notices on their sides that proclaimed: 'This is now a Red Bus', as 920 demonstrates. It was waiting to depart from The Strand – Barnstaple's bus station from the 1920s until the late 1990s – on a damp day in 1983. Later re-registered ADV 435A, it was withdrawn in 1986.

THE VEHICLES NORTH Devon (Red Bus) received from Western National were mainly the usual NBC mix of Bristol saloons and deckers (LHs, REs and VRs) and Leyland Leopard coaches. The minibus revolution could not come quickly enough, and a start was made in 1983 with the acquisition of the first of seven Iveco 35-8 fourteen-seater van conversions by Potteries, 4 (A329 GBF), also photographed at the Strand bus station, Barnstaple. These vehicles pioneered the use of the red and yellow livery and 'Little Red Bus' fleetname and were used extensively on Barnstaple town services, although they also saw service as National Holidays' feeders. At this time, the livery on 4 has been augmented by advertising for Brian Ford's Discount Centre.

MOVING NEXT TO BIDEFORD, at the southern end of the Quay lies the Grade I listed Long Bridge, aptly named as at 222 yards it is one of the longest medieval bridges in England, dating back to the thirteenth century. The scene is captured beautifully on this mid-1920s' postcard, which carries a blind stamp in the bottom right-hand corner identifying the publisher as W. H. Friendship of Bideford. In the foreground, a Leyland G7 is bound for Barnstaple, and will shortly turn left into the village of East-the-Water. TA 9879 was new to Colwills (Ilfracombe) Ltd in 1924; it was among the last of five vehicles received before the business passed to Hardy Central Garage (trading as Hardy-Colwills) in July that year. It went to National in 1927, gaining the fleet number 2461, but appears not to have made the transition to Southern National two years later. But no matter; there is so much period detail here in which also to revel – the horses and carts (Mr Chaplin's, immediately behind the bus, is particularly grand), the fashions of the time, and the splendid marble bust of John Richard Pine-Coffin (1842–90), a local politician, which still stands in those grounds today.

BIDEFORD'S LONG BRIDGE, photographed in 2019. Just visible in the distance is the modern bridge that now carries the A39.

W. H. FRIENDSHIP, BIDEFORD.

THERE WAS SOME surprise when in 2000/01 First Red Bus received eleven Alexander AL-bodied Leyland Atlanteans from Aberdeen, almost 600 miles away! All were getting on for 20 years old when they arrived, and little was done to improve their appearance. Ostensibly a short-term solution to assist in the withdrawal of Bristol VRs, many of which were equally old, they were all withdrawn between 2004 and 2005, but in June 2001, the oldest of them all, 1011 (NRS 307W), was on the bridge, heading towards Bideford but ultimately bound for Appledore.

APPLEDORE SITS ON the opposite side of the Taw and Torridge estuary from Instow, a few miles north of Bideford. The terminus for the 2 was on the quay, outside the Seagate Hotel, and in practice this required drivers to turn and wait for time in the nearby car park, with its superb view over the water. Dennis Dart SLF/Plaxton 4011 (N612 WND) was doing precisely that in this scene in June 2000. It was still in dealer white livery following its acquisition from Western Buses (AA) in 1998. The route was initially the 116 from Bideford only; it took until the 1980s for it to be extended at the eastern end to Braunton. North Devon (Red Bus) split the route, running Barnstaple to Westward Ho! as the 1; to Appledore as the 2; and to Ilfracombe as the 3; but in 2000, the 3 was withdrawn, leaving the 1, and some journeys on the 2, to serve Ilfracombe again.

THE BEACH AT Westward Ho! extends for 3 miles, and the area is another that is popular with surfers. There once was a railway – the Bideford, Westward Ho! and Appledore – which functioned for a mere sixteen years (1901–17) and was not connected at any point to the rest of the network. The Path utilises part of the old track bed. On 10 June 2019, I had gone to Westward Ho! for a shot of a Stagecoach South West vehicle on the 21 but parked up in Nelson Road, awaiting the departure time of 08:45 was BV17 GSY, a Volvo B11RT/Caetano Levante with Edwards Coaches of Bristol. With stops of 30 minutes or more at Bristol, Birmingham and Leicester, National Express service 339 was not due to arrive in Grimsby until 21:05.

A NUMBER OF Bristol MW6Gs made their way to Western National from Mansfield District and Bristol Omnibus in 1973/74. 3002 (267 HNU) came from the former, and its ECW body was repainted into green and white local coach livery, appropriately, given its dual purpose status. At the time, several of Western National's former MWs from the Royal Blue fleet were also undergoing conversion to bus or DP status. 3002 was photographed on the steady climb out of Clovelly on the 319 service to Hartland; allocated to St Austell until its final few months of service, which were performed at Bideford, it was withdrawn in November 1977. (Martin Llewelyn/Omnicolour)

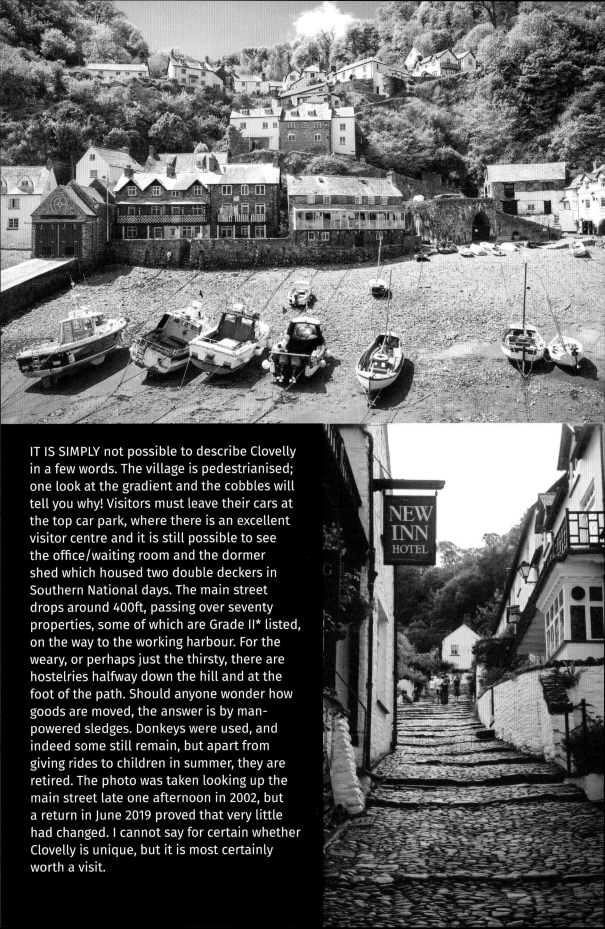

IT IS SIMPLY not possible to describe Clovelly in a few words. The village is pedestrianised; one look at the gradient and the cobbles will tell you why! Visitors must leave their cars at the top car park, where there is an excellent visitor centre and it is still possible to see the office/waiting room and the dormer shed which housed two double deckers in Southern National days. The main street drops around 400ft, passing over seventy properties, some of which are Grade II* listed, on the way to the working harbour. For the weary, or perhaps just the thirsty, there are hostelries halfway down the hill and at the foot of the path. Should anyone wonder how goods are moved, the answer is by man-powered sledges. Donkeys were used, and indeed some still remain, but apart from giving rides to children in summer, they are retired. The photo was taken looking up the main street late one afternoon in 2002, but a return in June 2019 proved that very little had changed. I cannot say for certain whether Clovelly is unique, but it is most certainly worth a visit.

FROM CLOVELLY, THE Path leads to Hartland Point, where a sharp left turn takes the walker to Hartland Quay. There is no bus service here; the nearest is once again the 319, which calls at Hartland village. The Hartland–Bude section was dropped in the 1970s, and there have been various permutations of service levels since then. In 2000, First Western National offered two trips as the 119 between Bude and Hartland, and First Red Bus ran the main 319 service, which was now extended to Barnstaple. One such journey was the 07:50 and 16:10 return to and from the North Devon College, which was numbered X19, and on 23 June this was in the hands of Red Bus Leyland National 2814 (RJT 148R), which has just discharged its final passengers at Northgate Green, Hartland. 2814 had recently been transferred in from First Hampshire (though its livery is that of Provincial); it was withdrawn the following year, but the X19 disappeared at the start of the 2000 autumn term.

THE 219, PROVIDED by Stagecoach South West, is now the principal service between Hartland and Bude, with five departures on most weekdays, and brings us to the Strand in the centre of the town. Bude's transport history over the last fifty years might be described as topsy-turvy. Western National sold its depot there to local coach owner Jennings in 1971. It returned in the 1990s, but when First pulled out of north Cornwall in 2003, retaining just its express services, it was Summercourt-based operator Western Greyhound that stepped in. Plymouth Citybus, part of the Go-Ahead group, bought Western Greyhound's Liskeard operations in 2014, and rebranded them as Go Cornwall. As of 2019, the company has sixteen routes that run wholly or partly in Cornwall, one of which is the 12B, the extension of the 12 from Launceston. Volvo B7RLE/Wright Eclipse 2 102 (WA12 ACU) has recently arrived in Bude, but it should be noted that its 'Blue Flash' livery is appropriate to the 11/A/B (Bodmin and Padstow).

THE FINAL LEG on this stage of the journey is the 15 miles between Bude and Boscastle. Following the demise of Western Greyhound, First Kernow – what remained of the Cornish operations of First Devon & Cornwall – increased its presence in the area it had abandoned in 2003, and it provides our next link with the 95 (Bude–St Columb Major). Boscastle is a charming village which includes amongst its many attractions a Museum of Witchcraft and Magic, and a picturesque harbour. In August 2004, it was hit by a flash flood which caused extensive damage – fifty-two years to the day since Lynmouth's flood – though fortunately no lives were lost. Four years earlier, on 23 June, Dennis Dart SLF 4434 (P434 ORL) is about to cross the bridge over the River Jordan on Penally Hill, on its way to take up a school journey.

Boscastle.

Boscastle to Newquay: 50 Miles

Total so far: 190 miles

On this section

The Path passes the site of the ruined castle at Tintagel. After a further 9 miles Port Isaac is reached. A typical Cornish fishing village, it occupies a delightful position on the bay. Next is Polzeath, another surfers' hotspot, before we arrive in Rock, which, as it sits on the opposite bank of the River Camel to Padstow, necessitates a ferry journey; the first of several such crossings required in order to complete the walk without resorting to lengthy detours. It is 17 miles from here to Newquay by road, though 23 along the Path; such is the nature of this section of coastline. At Trevone, there is a large blow hole, where a cave once collapsed into the sea; Mawgan Porth and Watergate Bay are two more locations popular with surfers. It is fair to say, however, that where surfing is concerned, most people will think of Newquay, a leading tourist destination for well over a century.

A view to Tintagel island, showing the Tintagel castle ruins and Merlin's cave on the shoreline.

Things to see

No sooner have we left Boscastle than we are plunged into the world of Arthurian legend. A cantilever bridge, opened in 2019, allows easier access to the Tintagel Castle site. Archaeologists have found evidence of remains in the area dating back to late Roman times. Port Isaac has featured on television several times, most notably as the setting for the ITV series *Doc Martin*.

Rock is the location of the Doom Bar, a sandbank which has caused many shipwrecks over the years, and is the name given to a popular ale first brewed here. Over the water, Padstow might be

Padstow harbour.

regarded as the gastronomical capital of Cornwall, since renowned chefs Rick Stein and Paul Ainsworth each have several businesses here. Parking spaces at this busy resort are soon filled, and a park-and-ride service now operates in summer months. Midway between Padstow and Newquay, Bedruthan Steps boasts golden sands and massive granite rocks and stacks, which, according to legend, were stepping stones for a giant.

The blessing of Newquay's west-facing position has brought major international surfing competitions – there is even a surf museum – in recent years. But there are plenty of other things to see and do, including the zoo, the Blue Reef Aquarium and Pirate's Quest.

Bedruthan Steps, granite rocks and stacks stand on the golden beach.

Towan Beach, Newquay.

An outline of bus services past...

National, and from 1929 Southern National, were the principal service providers along this part of the coast. Western National assumed responsibility in NBC days and beyond, although under FirstGroup management it pulled out of most of north Cornwall from 2001 onwards, paving the way for independent Western Greyhound to build up a substantial network. The old and much-photographed bus station and travel centre at East Street closed in 2004, and services now depart from a purpose-built replacement in Manor Road. Since 2015, First Kernow has been the predominant operator.

...and present

Bus routes along this section of the Path tend to be quite lengthy affairs but do mostly stick to the coast roads. This entire section is covered by First Kernow:

- continue on service 95 from Boscastle to Slaughter Bridge
- service 55 (from Bodmin Parkway) links Slaughter Bridge and Delabole
- service 96 links Delabole with Port Isaac, Polzeath and Rock use the ferry crossing to Padstow
- service A5 links Padstow with Trenance, Mawgan Porth and Newquay. This route is part of the Atlantic Coasters network, so a trip on an open-top bus might be feasible in good weather.

FROM THE DIRECTION of Camelford, Port Isaac is approached along a narrow, twisting road with few passing places, which may account for why the driver of Western Greyhound Mercedes O814D Vario/Plaxton 531 (V31 WGL) was running around 10 minutes late. He also may not have been expecting a photographer as he launched his vehicle at this almost 90 degree bend in the centre of the village. Western Greyhound took the service on in 2003, when First Western National abandoned its north Cornwall network and ran it as Camelford and Wadebridge. It had been the 124 Boscastle–Wadebridge previously. Port Isaac is the location for the popular ITV series *Doc Martin*, and although it was not being filmed at the time of this August 2010 visit, there were still a fair few tourists around to take in the sights.

ROCK STANDS ON the River Camel estuary, opposite Padstow, and has seen a huge surge in popularity in the past thirty years. It is reckoned to have the highest proportion of second homes in Cornwall, and has been dubbed by the *Daily Telegraph* as both the 'Kensington of Cornwall' and 'Chelsea-on-Sea'. The Princes William and Harry were regular visitors during their teenage years. Problems for visitors included the usual narrow roads and the lack of parking spaces, so a seasonal park-and-ride service was instituted, and in the mid-1990s, it was being operated by one of Western National's Carlyle-bodied Mercedes 811Ds, 321 (H721 HGL).

IN PADSTOW, MUCH of the riverside walk and beyond, past the old railway station, is nowadays given over to car parks, such is the popularity of the town. The line closed on 30 January 1967, but the building is still intact. The A5 is now the main route to Newquay, and about to depart from the bus stand is First Kernow 33141 (LR02 LWW), a Transbus Trident that began life in 2002 in London as TN1141, working out of Greenford depot. It has received advertising livery for Vamooz, the free app that allows intending passengers to suggest trips and book seats, introduced into Cornwall in 2018.

THE COACH BAYS in the parking area at Padstow usually contain something of interest, and the empty space allowed a nice offside view of Shearings Grand Tourer 832 (BF16 XDS), a Mercedes-Benz tri-axle Tourismo, on 10 May 2017. The windscreen notice suggests that it is on a day outing from its holiday base in St Mawes. This is another location we will meet as we continue along the Path, but not for another 168 miles!

THE WESTERN AND Southern National companies were enthusiastic users of the Bristol SU, taking 133 of the approximately 180 produced. The first sixteen, the SUS4A, seated thirty; the later SUL4As thirty-six – or thirty-three as coaches. Received in five batches between 1960 and 1966, these attractive vehicles were well-suited to the narrow roads of Cornwall and Devon; service lives of over ten years were not uncommon. This is 668 (BDV 249C), climbing out of Trenance on its way to Newquay from Padstow on the 171 (the predecessor of the 56, 556 and A5). The photo dates from the late 1960s; by 1970, 668 had migrated eastwards to Taunton. It was withdrawn in June 1978.

BY 1977, WESTERN National's open-top fleet, mainly inherited from Devon General and consisting of two 1957 vintage Bristol LDLs, the nine 'Sea Dog' Atlanteans from 1961 and a pair of AEC Regent Vs, new in 1964, was becoming somewhat long in the tooth. So between October 1977 and January 1978, eleven new convertible open-top VR3s arrived, named after warships to maintain the naval connection and with fleet numbers 934–44 that followed on from the Atlanteans. The first nine were allocated to Torquay, the last two to Falmouth and Penzance respectively. When Devon General and Southern National became separate entities again in 1983, Western National was left with just four: 937, 941, 943 and 944, and it is the first of these, 937 (VDV 137S), 'Victory', which was seen on 9 August 1984 in Marcus Hill, Newquay, on the 56 from Padstow. It was transferred to Badgerline in 1990, and following retirement in early 2005, it was acquired by the Western Historic Omnibus & Transport Trust for preservation.

THE TRAVEL CENTRE at East Street is partially obscured by First Western National 1140 (AFJ 705T), as it loads for the 13:25 to Wadebridge, the only one of the three weekday departures to venture beyond Padstow. Interestingly, the timetable points out that there would be no regular Saturday service, but instead an 'excursion' coach would leave Newquay at 12:00, subject to demand. Sunday was clearly the best day to travel, with four return journeys to Wadebridge, starting from there at 09:45. 1140 carries an attractive overall advertisement for the RAF, with a different design on the nearside. It was one of three buses to do so, later examples being Leyland Olympian 1755 and Volvo Citybus 38009.

THE WESTERN GREYHOUND fleet grew from three when it was founded to eighteen just twelve months later (January 1999), including the first of the Mercedes Varios which, thanks to the sheer numbers operated, are most associated with the company. Three double deckers arrived in mid-2000, and although this was the third of them, it was numbered 1 (VOD 596S); it came from Stagecoach Cheltenham (218) but was new to Devon General (576). Withdrawal was not far away when this photo was taken at the future site of Newquay bus station, as good second-hand Olympians were becoming available. And the pink and white livery would also soon be replaced, as when First introduced its corporate pink 'Barbie' scheme, Western Greyhound progressively switched to green and white – the colours of the old Western National.

AT 01:00 ON 13 May 2013, a fire – believed to have been started deliberately – broke out at Western Greyhound's Summercourt depot. Thirty-four buses, with a value approaching £1.5 million, were destroyed. Services were disrupted for a time, but it was heartening that nine other operators, some as far away as Blackpool, arranged the immediate hire of vehicles to cover the losses. Summercourt Travel, whose base was next door to Western Greyhound, helped out with WDZ 1033 (*L815 NNW*), a Dennis Lance with Alexander Strider bodywork that was new in 1993 as Yorkshire Woollen 815. It was seen soon afterwards in St George's Street, turning into Manor Road where the new bus station is situated, having worked the 559 from Trencreek.

Newquay to St Just: 60 Miles
Total so far: 250 miles

On this section

The characteristics of this section of the north Cornwall coast vary little until St Ives Bay is reached. Sandy beaches grace small, delightful holiday resorts: Perranporth, St Agnes, Portreath. Copper and tin mining was prevalent in the area until the 1920s. Godrevy Island marks the start of the bay and from here, the Path follows the beach until it reaches Hayle – at the point where the railway crosses the main road on an imposing viaduct. It continues along the western side of the bay until it reaches St Ives. From here to Cape Cornwall, however, the scene changes dramatically. There are no settlements of any size until reaching St Just (which is about one mile inland). High cliffs and moorland dominate. The Carracks are a group of rocky islands, home to seal families, while Pendeen Watch is a lighthouse, built in 1900.

Godrevy Island.

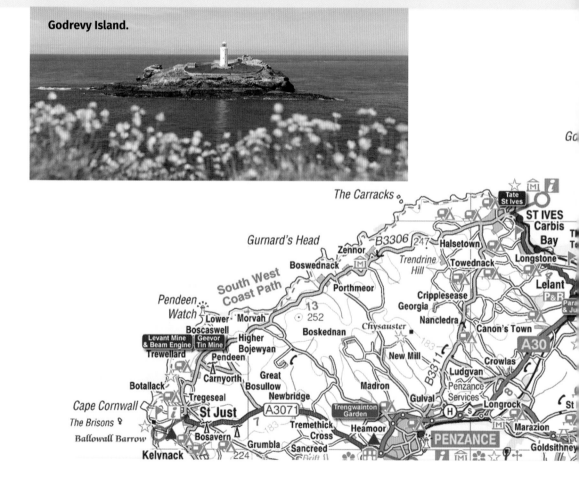

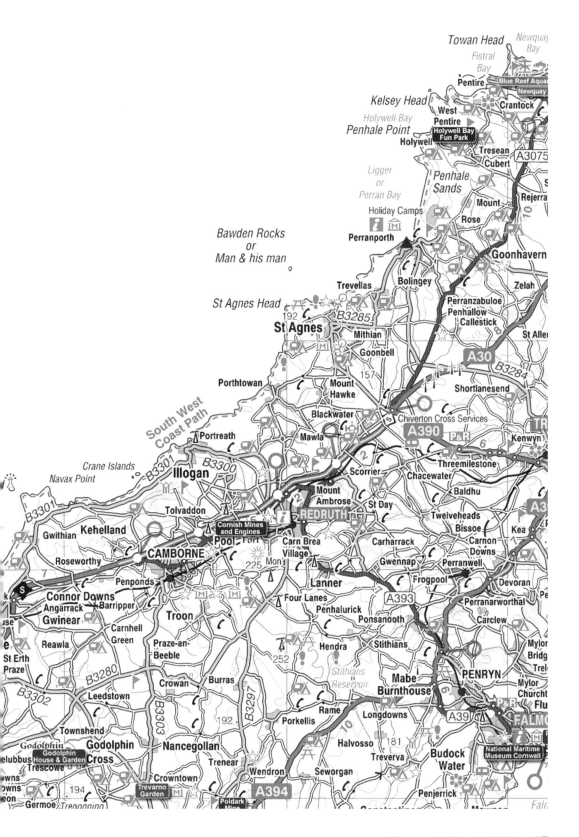

Fistral Beach.

Fistral Beach, on the west side of Newquay, is exposed to Atlantic swells which produce consistently good waves that can on occasion reach a height of 30ft. Not so when I took this photo in July 2002, but one or two hardy souls were still enjoying the water.

Things to see

Winston Graham, author of the Poldark novels, lived in Perranporth for many years. The town hosts a sea-song and shanty festival every April and a surf triathlon each September. The first Cornish railway, the Portreath Tramroad, opened in 1809, using horse-drawn wagons to link the tin mining areas with the harbour.

St Ives has always had a strong link with the art world, and it is often said that the quality of the light here is exceptional. The Tate St Ives gallery and Barbara Hepworth Museum are a must for any visitor, but there is much enjoyment to be had wandering the narrow streets and indulging in some retail therapy.

View of St Ives town and harbour.

An outline of bus services past...

Devon Motor Transport, through its takeover of Cornwall Enterprise Motors of Perranporth in 1923, established a network of services in the Truro and Falmouth area, which expanded across large parts of Cornwall as new routes were started and other acquisitions made. The name Cornwall Motor Services (CMT) was adopted for operations in the county, but National acquired the business in 1928. Newquay marked the north coast boundary where Southern National's services ended and Western National's began. First Kernow is now firmly back in charge in the area after the Western Greyhound interregnum.

...and present

In 2019, the best time to have undertaken the route would have been between 7 July and 31 August, the operating dates of the Atlantic Coaster A4 from Newquay to St Ives, which follows the route of the Path quite closely. Otherwise:

- service 87 links Newquay with Threemilestone
- service T2 links Threemilestone with St Ives...
...but they only follow the Path to St Agnes and from Hayle.
- service A3 links St Ives with St Just
All services are operated by First Kernow.

For the first time, main line rail connections with places served by the Path are possible. GWR operates several services each day between Par and Newquay, and St Erth and St Ives.

FIRST KERNOW LIVERY owes much to that designed for use by The Buses of Somerset – also part of First South West – and the two-tone green is a welcome improvement on corporate livery. It is seen to good effect on Alexander-Dennis Enviro 33309 (WK18 CGF) as it leaves the turning circle in Perranporth on its way to Newquay on 10 June 2019. The 87 is one of six services linking Newquay and Truro by different routes.

TIMETABLES FOR THE 44 and 46 services to Portreath show the terminus as 'Beach', and clearly Mercedes L608D/Robin Hood 134 (C985 GCV) could not get much nearer on a sunny September day in 1993. It carries the attractive blue, red and cream livery introduced after the Badgerline group took majority control of Western National in 1988; the 'Hoppa' name dates back to minibus introduction three years earlier, and had been largely phased out by this time. As was the company's wont in those days, letter suffixes indicating route variations were commonplace, and the 1993 summer timetable lists a 44, 44A, 44B and 44C for the service from Camborne. Redruth had to make do with the 46B; there was no 46 or 46A! 134 had less than a year left in Cornwall; it was transferred to Badgerline as its 4711 in 1994.

THE PATH PASSES behind and to the left, as we look at it, of the imposing viaduct that dominates the town. It was built in 1852; the original wooden supports were later replaced by the stone pillars we see today, although the railway first came to Hayle some fifteen years earlier to service local industries connected with mining. Arriving in Foundry Square on 20 June 2000 was Dennis Dart SLF/Plaxton Pointer 2 4457 (R457 CCV), on its way to St Ives. The 14 and 14D ran at hourly intervals, the difference being that the 14D did not call at St Erth.

STILL IN HAYLE on the same day, Plaxton Expressliner 2-bodied Volvo B10M 2308 (R308 JAF) is nearing the end of its journey from Edinburgh. Unusually, National Express allowed advertising (other than their own) on vehicles used on their contracts; this was in aid of the McDonalds 'Our Town Story' project, in which each local education authority had been invited to create a show around the people and places in their area, to be performed at the newly opened Millennium Dome.

DESCRIBED IN TIMETABLES as 'one of the most scenic routes in Britain', the 15 followed the coast on its 90-minute journey from St Ives to Land's End. It was also advertised as an open-top bus route, although there was a warning that it might not always be operated with one. That seems to have been the case on this occasion, when quite a crowd are waiting to board 1239 (UAR 595W), a Bristol VR3/ECW transferred to Western National from Thamesway in August 1992. St Ives bus station – known as The Malakoff because it resembles the redoubt of that name in the Crimea and whose building in the early 1930s caused Western National a considerable amount of difficulty – provides wonderful views across the bay.

MERCEDES 811D/PLAXTON 341 (K341 OAF) demonstrates how little room there is for anything much wider than a car in St Ives. It was making its way up Tregenna Hill on its way to the Malakoff, having worked in from Penzance on the 16. New in December 1992, it carries blue and white livery with a band of blue and red flags and, facing forwards behind the rear wheel arch, a smiling badger, denoting ownership by the Badgerline group.

THE ACQUISITION OF the Grenville business by Western National in March 1988 brought over thirty vehicles into the fleet, ranging in age from an Albion Nimbus and a pair of former Plymouth Atlanteans (new in 1963 and 1966 respectively) to a Volvo B10M/ Duple from 1984, which Grenville had acquired from Ferris, Senghenydd (near Caerphilly). This became Western National 2239 (A747 JAY), and turned out to be something of a survivor, as it was not withdrawn and sold until November 1996. In this July 1988 photograph, it can be seen entering the car and coach park in St Ives; a welcome place to leave one's vehicle for a meander around the town, with its narrow and often heavily congested streets, either on foot or, for the less brave, on the frequent park-and-ride service. 2239 has yet to receive its Western National fleet number plate, and it was destined to carry Grenville of Cornwall fleetnames until July 1995.

IN TERMS OF the Path, this section should end at Cape Cornwall, but a mile inland is the small town of St Just. There is an hourly daytime service on the A17, another of the Atlantic Coasters that runs from Pendeen via St Just to Penzance and then to St Ives. Going back to 1993, there were four routes to Penzance (10, 10A, 10B and 11) but the only link with St Ives was the summer open-top 15, which continues today as the A1 (Penzance–Land's End–St Ives). Awaiting departure time at 13:17 on 10 June 2019 was one of the older members of the First Kernow fleet, Transbus Trident/ Transbus President 33233 (HIG 1528, LT52 WWV), which was new to First London (TN1233) at Westbourne Park.

Clock Tower in St. Just,
Cornwall.

St Just to Falmouth: 84 Miles
Total so far: 334 miles

On this section

Sennen Cove is the first notable settlement on this stretch of the Path and is another coastal village popular with surfers. From here, it is only a short journey to Land's End. The Path now starts its long journey eastwards along the south coast, via Porthcurno, Lamorna, Mousehole and Newlyn, to Penzance. The largest town in the area, Penzance is home to the most southerly railway station in England, the terminus of the Great Western line from Paddington. Marazion is the starting point for visits to St Michael's Mount. After Praa Sands comes Porthleven, a fishing port said to be the most southerly in mainland Britain and another surfers' favourite. Kynance Cove is one of the most beautiful along this stretch of coastline. Lizard town is about half a mile inland from Lizard Point. The halfway point of the Path is reached at Porthallow. There are two ferry journeys on the final run to Falmouth; the one at Gillan Creek is a shortcut, and the Helford River ferry is seasonal; the detour if it is not running adds a day (13 miles) to a walker's itinerary. The final 10 miles into Falmouth provide excellent views of Pendennis Point and Falmouth Bay.

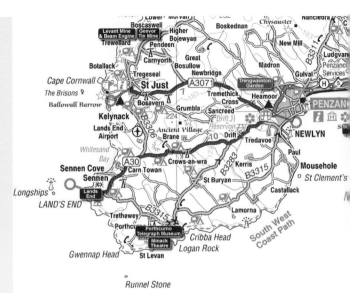

Sennen Cove.

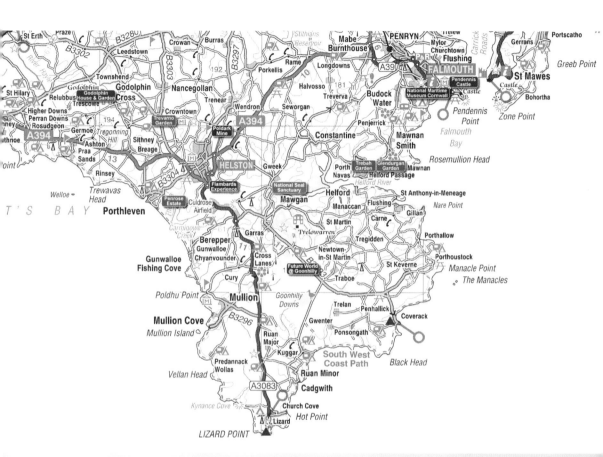

Penzance station in June 2019. On the right is one of the new Class 802 bi-mode sets, 802 113, newly introduced into service. On the left, 43 170, one of several short sets that are replacing DMUs. Both are operated by GWR.

Things to see

Land's End was owned by a Cornish family until 1982. It has since been developed as a theme park. It is the most westerly point in England and is the starting – or finishing – place for charity walks, bike rides, even bus journeys, to – or from – John O'Groats, a distance of around 875 miles. Porthcurno is worth a visit for the Minack open-air theatre and the telegraph museum; it was in Porthcurno that a famous international submarine communications cable station was set up in the 1870s.

Mousehole is a pretty fishing village to which people will travel miles each December to see the Christmas illuminations. Newlyn is said to be the last place the *Mayflower* visited in 1620 before it set sail for America, and the 1880s saw the birth of the Newlyn School of painters.

Minack open-air theatre with Porthcurno beach in the background.

Mousehole.

The passenger ferry to the Isles of Scilly leaves from the Penzance harbour, and there was a helicopter service to the islands, but that closed in 2012. The Path stays close to the sea until it reaches Marazion. From here, it is possible at low tide to walk across the causeway to St Michael's Mount. Managed by the National Trust, it is well worth a visit (and there is a boat on which to travel should the tide turn).

The halfway way point of the Path – 315 miles (507km) is reached at Porthallow.

Falmouth has five beaches, the National Maritime Museum, a sixteenth-century fort, Pendennis Castle (built by Henry VIII), and at Mawnan Smith, Trebah Gardens, described as 'one of the great gardens of Cornwall'.

Pendennis Castle.

Trebah Gardens.

An outline of bus services past...

CMT, National, Western National, Western Greyhound and First Kernow have been the principal operators over the years, though it must not be forgotten that this was also Great Western Railway territory, and it ran the first recorded motor bus service from Helston to Lizard on 17 August 1903.

...and present

Most of this section of the Path is reasonably well shadowed by the following First Kernow services:

- service A3 links St Just with Sennen Cove, Land's End, Porthcurno and Newlyn
- service M6 links Newlyn with Mousehole; return to Penzance
- service U4 links Penzance with Marazion and Porthleven; then continue to Helston
- service L1 links Helston with The Lizard; service L2 links Helston with Coverack and St Keverne
- service 323, provided by OTS, links St Keverne with Helford. However, it only operates once a day and requires a ferry crossing to Helford Passage, so an easier alternative would be to return to Helston or RNAS Culdrose for First Kernow 35, which provides the link with Helford Passage, Mawnan Smith and Falmouth.

WESTERN NATIONAL RECEIVED 15 Bristol VR3s – the VDV ***S registered class – between November 1977 and March 1978, of which the batch numbered 1114–1121 were particularly interesting. They were allocated initially to Plymouth, but after a few years' service there they were all despatched to Cornwall, split between St Austell and Camborne depots, where they remained until withdrawal. Several were given advertising liveries during this time; this is 1114 (VDV 114S) on 30 July 1997 in the later of two schemes for Pirate FM, a commercial radio station based in Redruth. It was climbing away from Sennen Cove, something that even a VR had to undertake in low gear, on a 1B working back from Land's End back to Penzance. The waves crashing over the rocks in the background, known as The Tribbens, are quite spectacular.

THE BRISTOL LD6B was designed as a replacement for the K and for a low height double decker it was remarkable in having centre gangways on both decks (instead of one along the offside upstairs). The first to arrive was 1863 (OTT 2), in 1953, and when this photo was taken, in or around 1969, the Penzance–Land's End route, for many years the 1, had become the 501. Western National maintained an outstation at Land's End for many years, and 1863, already well laden for the return to Penzance, is standing outside it. A Grey Cars coach in the background completes the scene, and proves the point that even in the days before the theme park, significant numbers of tourists were attracted to the place.

FEW PHOTOS I have ever seen of buses at Mousehole convey the narrowness of the streets that bus drivers have to contend with as well as this one. 1565 (KRL 444W) was a Bristol LHS6L with Wadham Stringer bodywork new to N. R. Harvey & Sons, who were based in the village, in 1981. In 1986, their business passed to Grenville Motors of Camborne, which in turn was acquired by Western National in 1988. The two ex-Harvey vehicles were given the traditional blue and cream livery and Blue Bus fleetnames – a nice touch.

THE TRACKSIDE VIEW of Penzance station featured in the
introduction to this section. This photo shows part of the station
building itself, which was opened in 1879 to replace the original
wooden structure that had been destroyed in a fire three years
earlier. The bus station is sited next to the railway, making this
area a true interchange; it was opened in July 1968, and is where
Western National's Bristol LH6L/ECW 1623 (KTT 46P), new in
1975, is heading. The 535 linked Penzance with Falmouth, where
1623 was allocated; the service originated with National, who
numbered it 263.

THE SUN ISN'T always shining in the south-west; on this July day in 1986 it was particularly dull and wet. With the railway station in the background, two of Western National's newer buses awaited their next tour of duty in Penzance bus station. 67 (C682 ECV) was a Reeves Burgess-bodied Mercedes L608D with Penzance Hoppa fleetnames, new the previous year. Coach-seated Leyland Olympian/ECW 1800 (A750 VAF) was employed on the Cornwall X1 express service to Plymouth, a new initiative, linking Plymouth with either Newquay and Perranporth or Penzance. Both carry the livery, introduced with the minibuses, that was spelling the end for National Bus Company leaf green.

IN RECENT YEARS, the bus station has been restructured and refurbished. Loading on outbound services now takes place on the opposite side of the central island; new arrivals use this side to offload their passengers, and out of service vehicles park up on the far side, against the sea wall. First Kernow Volvo B7TL/Plaxton President 32208 (HIG 8790, *LT52 WTO*) is another to have made its way here from First London, this time via Eastern Counties. It is one of six to have had a partial open-top conversion on arrival, and for all its 16 plus years, it looked very smart in Atlantic Coasters' livery, having just run in on the A2 from St Ives in June 2019.

BACK TO THE 1970s now for photos of two Western National vehicles at Marazion (Square), the dropping off point for a visit to St Michael's Mount. This is Leyland Atlantean/MCW 987 (504 DKT), one of almost forty veterans drafted in from PMT, Trent, or in this case, Maidstone & District, to assist with conversion to one-person operation. It arrived in 1976, and was withdrawn in May 1981. (Tony Thorne/Omnicolour)

BRISTOL LDL6G/ECW 1936 (VDV 753) 'Sir Humphry Davy', a 1957 example converted to open-top in 1973 (to match sister 1935, which was so treated the previous year), and also looking in good condition in the white and green dual-purpose style livery used for these vehicles in NBC days. It was withdrawn in March 1979, moving to Eastern Counties. (Martin Llewelyn/Omnicolour)

THE PENZANCE–HELSTON–FALMOUTH route was numbered 2 in the 1980s and so it remained until September 2017, when the link with Falmouth was broken, services continuing from Helston only as far as Penryn Campus. It was renumbered U4, and a significant vehicle upgrade saw the introduction of ADL E40Ds in this attractive two-tone blue dedicated livery, which also covers their use on the U1 and U2, linking the Campus with Truro and Redruth respectively. 33471 (WK66 BYV) was spotted in Porthleven on 10 June 2019.

TRURONIAN WAS FOUNDED in 1987 by three former Western National managers who had lost out to Plympton Coachlines/Badgerline when their company was privatised. It grew quite quickly, with the acquisition of Flora Motors, and Roseland Motors' Veryan–Truro route, tendering gains and excursions, holidays and private hire work. Certain routes were named: the T3 was the 'Lizard Rambler', the T9 the 'Eden Branch Line', while the T34, between RNAS Culdrose and Redruth, became 'The Helston Branch Line'. But the longest, at 2½ hours, the T1, joined the north and south coasts, working from Perranporth to Lizard, and this is the duty Dennis Dart SLF/Plaxton Pointer 2 T35 JCV was undertaking on Sunday, 17 August 2003, when celebrations for the hundredth anniversary of the first GWR bus service from Helston to the Lizard were taking place. Truronian carried on until April 2008, when it was sold to First and the fleet merged with that of First Devon & Cornwall.

THIS BEAUTIFUL STUDY of village life appears on a postcard whose provenance is unknown. It features a Thorneycroft A1 with Vickers twenty-four-seat bodywork, whose driver poses self-consciously in front of his vehicle. Two passengers have already 'bagged' the front nearside seats, and the children of the village watch the proceedings from across the road. The route to Falmouth was National's 236A, becoming Western National's 42 in 1929; the bus was new to Devon Motor Transport, passing to National in 1928 and then Western National, who numbered it 2702 (CO 9342). This is Port Navas, or nowadays Porth Navas, which is part of an alternative route on the Path should the Helford ferry be non-operational.

AFTER HAVING AMASSED 2,646 Daimler/Leyland Fleetlines, London Transport decided in 1976 that the type was not wholly suitable for work in the capital, and withdrawals began in 1979. Western National was one of several operators pleased to snap them up, and during 1980 and 1981, built up a collection of thirty-eight. They were put to work in Cornwall, replacing aged Atlanteans that had come from Maidstone & District in the mid-1970s. In this photo dating from around 1984, Metro-Cammell-bodied 835 (THM 648M), the former DMS1648, was waiting in The Moor, Falmouth, before returning to Truro. The type were progressively withdrawn from 1983 onwards, with 835 moving to Midland Red (North) in July 1986.

IT WAS GENERAL election time when I visited Falmouth in June 2001, and across from The Moor in Berkeley Vale, Julian Brazil was on the campaign trail for the Liberal Democrats. Williams Travel of Camborne had supplied him with Volvo B10M/Jonckheere Jubilee B710 EOF, new to Flights in 1985. Mr Brazil was out of luck on polling day, finishing third behind Labour and the Conservatives.

6

Falmouth to Plymouth (Jennycliff Bay): 85 Miles

Total so far: 419 miles

On this section

Ferries are required to get us from Falmouth to St Mawes, and from there to Place, although the bus from St Mawes to Portscatho is a viable alternative. From here to Gorran Haven is quite a remote section of the Path, as it passes through a number of small villages, along relatively high cliffs. At Gorran Haven there is a community bus service (gorranbus.org.uk). Two miles further east is Mevagissey, a fishing port named after two Irish saints, St Meva and St Issey, which can trace its recorded history at least as far back as the early fourteenth century. It is connected to St Austell, the third largest town in Cornwall, by an hourly bus service. Another ferry crossing is required at Fowey, a picturesque little town at the mouth of the river. Looe is divided into two parts, East and West, and along with nearby neighbours Hannafore and Seaton, caters for the holiday trade. Tregantle Fort is one of several built around Plymouth in the 1850s to deter attacks on its naval bases. At Cremyll, there is a passenger ferry across the River Tamar to Plymouth. This section ends at Jennycliff, south-east of the city.

Gorran Haven.

Mevagissey harbour.

Charlestown Harbour at low water.

Things to see

The area between St Mawes and Mevagissey is sparsely populated and short of tourist attractions, though there are a number of excellent botanical gardens further inland, including the Lost Gardens of Heligan. The docks at Charlestown, between St Austell and Par, have been used on many occasions as the setting for film and TV dramas, while nearby, the eponymous hotel at Carlyon Bay was the scene of a historic meeting between Tony Blair and

the Irish Taoiseach, Bertie Ahern, in 2000. Whilst historically the whole area is known for its china clay deposits, a reclaimed pit has become the famous Eden Project botanical garden, which opened in 2001.

Daphne du Maurier once lived at Fowey and is honoured by a festival every May. Polperro, set on a hillside like Clovelly and arguably as pretty, also repels the motor car, but only at certain times of the year.

The quaint fishing village of Polperro.

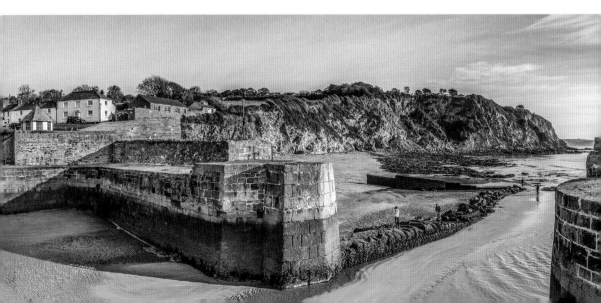

Mount Edgcumbe. Mount Edgcumbe is a Grade II listed stately home with a landscaped park and magnificent views across the Plymouth Sound. Once in Plymouth, the famous Hoe and Barbican are on the route of the Path.

A photo taken from Plymouth Hoe, looking out over Plymouth Sound. From here, as every good schoolchild was taught, Sir Francis Drake played bowls while waiting for the tide to turn before engaging with the Spanish Armada. In years past, both Plymouth Bus and the Western National Preservation Group held their annual rallies here, and it was in July 1998 that preserved Western National Bristol KS5G/ECW 994 (LTA 813) was climbing Hoe Road, loaded with visitors sampling one of the free rides on offer that day.

An outline of bus services past…

Devon Motor Transport, National and GWR were all active in east Cornwall until superseded by Western National in 1929. Plymouth Corporation Tramways Department, founded in 1892, was the forerunner of Plymouth City Transport, and later Plymouth Citybus. Good working arrangements with Western National, including many 'Joint Services', lasted from the time of the Second World War until the post-deregulation period, 1987/88. It is only in recent times, following the demise of Western Greyhound and First's withdrawal from the area, that Plymouth Citybus, now part of the Go-Ahead group, has moved into much of east and north Cornwall.

…and present

Along this section of the Path, services link the larger centres of population. Unlike north Cornwall, they go to the coast rather than follow it. After the ferry crossing to St Mawes:

- First Kernow service 50 links St Mawes and Portscatho with Probus; change to service 51 at Bessybeneath (on maps as Ruan High Lanes) to visit Portloe, which the Path passes
- First Kernow service 27 links Probus with St Austell
- Travel Cornwall service 471 links St Austell with Heligan Gardens and Gorran Haven, while First Kernow service 25 links St Austell with Mevagissey (southbound) and Carlyon Bay, Par and Fowey (eastbound)
- After the ferry from Fowey to Polruan, Travel Cornwall service 481 links Polruan with Polperro and Looe. Plymouth Citybus service 73 links Polperro and Looe with Liskeard
- Plymouth Citybus service 75 links Liskeard with Seaton and Torpoint
- Plymouth Citybus service 70 links Torpoint and Cremyll for the passenger ferry across the Tamar
- Walk to Stonehouse Bridge and take Plymouth Citybus service 34 into central Plymouth and 25 to visit the Barbican and Plymouth Hoe
- Target Travel service 54, the Bovisand Beach Bus which called at Jennycliff Bay, operated a daily summer timetable for Spring Bank Holiday week and between 20 July and 1 September in 2019

WESTERN NATIONAL OPENED up a route from Truro to St Mawes via the King Harry ferry – the 146 – in April 1935. The St Mawes section was added to the 51 (Truro–Portscatho) in 1959, but by the mid-1980s it was in the hands of Lidgey's Coaches, as the 267/288. It returned to the fold, and to its original number, in the 1990s. I sampled it on a dull June day in 2001; I was the only passenger for half the outward journey, and it seems there were none wanting to go back on Mercedes 811D/PMT Ami 6384 (H351 HRF).

MEVAGISSEY WAS ORIGINALLY served by the buses of GWR Motor Services, the route becoming the 60 when Western National appeared on the scene. When I first visited, in 2000, services ran down into the centre, where I took a picture of a Mercedes 608D in Church Street, a thoroughfare scarcely wider than the bus itself. But in 2018, given the increase in traffic, both vehicular and pedestrian, the terminus has been moved to Valley Road, and on 24 May 2018, brand new ADL E20D 44960 (WK18 BVM) was about to make the turn onto the bus stand. Between the start of 2015 and the time of writing (mid-2019), First Kernow has received over eighty new vehicles; that is a rate of replacement of around 40 per cent.

IN 1996, MY COLLEAGUES and I spent an extremely productive,
though hard-working, few months in our office in St Austell,
during which time we stayed at the Cliff Head Hotel in nearby
Carlyon Bay. On Friday, 7 June, our work for the week not
completed, we were obliged to stay on for an extra night. The
hotel staff moved us into a side room for dinner because
Western National managers were hosting their long service
awards dinner in the main area. Guests arrived on board both
Mercedes 709D 632 (L632 VCV), seen here in the background, or
more interestingly, 582 (M582 DAF), a Caetano-bodied Toyota
Coaster bought new the previous year but withdrawn after only
four years' work at the end of 1998. Vehicles in Roberts' livery
carried a blue and yellow flags, as opposed to red and blue for
the main fleet.

THE SMALL FISHING village of Fowey, which sits at the mouth of the river that bears its name, was originally served by GWR bus services, and subsequently by Western National, with the terminal at the Safe Harbour Hotel in Lostwithiel Street. But the coming of the minibus era allowed the service from St Austell, now the 24, to be extended to the Polruan ferry, and this entailed the use of the Esplanade. On 15 May 1996, I had very little room in which to take up an off-road position for the photograph, and was fully expecting one of the smaller Mercedes L608Ds to appear. But no; Mercedes 709D/Plaxton 628 (L628 VCV) was working the route, and I watched as the driver stopped and retracted both wing mirrors before squeezing the vehicle through. The Polruan ferry continued to feature on timetables in later years; in the 2000s both First Devon & Cornwall and Western Greyhound ran into Fowey, though the terminus reverted to the Safe Harbour Hotel.

THE NEXT STOP on the journey is Polperro. Prior to the opening of the Tamar Bridge in 1961, it was served by National, and later Western National, from Torpoint. In the 1960s and 1970s the service, now starting from Plymouth, was cut back to Looe, but the Polperro connection was reinstated during the 1980s and is now in the hands of Plymouth Citybus (Go Cornwall). The timing point is the Crumplehorn, a thirteenth-century inn seen in the background here, though the actual stop is in Langreek Road. On 11 June 2019, Transbus Dart 65 (WJ52 GOH) had just arrived and has a healthy load for the 85-minute return journey.

VEHICULAR ACCESS TO the centre of Polperro is restricted; some roads are little wider than footpaths, and cars are banned from those that are not during the summer season. So a large car park is provided at the top of the village, close to the Crumplehorn, from which the Polperro Tram Co. provides a service down to the harbour using Morrison Electricar fourteen-seater milk float conversions. REO 207L, 'Lizzie', was doing a brisk trade when I saw it, also on 11 June 2019. At one time it was possible to make the same journey on a horse-drawn bus, but that option ended in September 2010.

THIS IS EAST LOOE in around 1990, looking towards the entrance to the station – the terminus of the short and picturesque branch line from Liskeard. The photographer – not me on this occasion – has given the viewer so much more to look at than if it had been just a standard bus shot. There is the splendid house in the background; the abundance of trees; the young lady walking with her dog (maybe giving the man with the camera a slightly quizzical look) – all competing with the bus for attention. The vehicle in question is 1084 (HTC 728N), which was new to Bristol (5502); it moved to Badgerline in 1986, and was loaned to Western National in September 1988 before being taken permanently into stock a couple of months later.

NEW IN DECEMBER 1973, this is Western National Bristol LH6L/ECW 1589 (NFJ 589M), seen whilst still in the first flush of youth at Cremyll, having worked in from Torpoint on the 86. There is a ferry here as well as at Torpoint, but this one is for foot passengers only, and is the route followed by the Path on its way east. The 86 was subsumed into the Plymouth–Torpoint service during the 1980s, but before that 1589 had been sold, moving to G. K. Kinch of Barrow-on-Soar, Leicestershire in March 1983.

ONCE THE FERRY from Cremyll has docked we are back in Devon, and the Path wends its way along the waterfront, bringing it to Plymouth's famous Hoe. In 2000, Plymouth Citybus, whose normal livery was red and white, placed four Dennis Dart SLF/Plaxton Pointer saloons in service in this fetching green and yellow scheme. The Milehouse Park & Ride service, for which they were intended, called at the station and Royal Parade en route to the Hoe, and 201 (X201 CDV), climbing up Madeira Road, is nearing journey's end. The name 'Hoe' comes from the Anglo-Saxon hoh, meaning a sloping ridge or hill shaped like an inverted human heel.

IT IS POSSIBLE to take a shortcut on the ferry from Sutton Harbour to Mount Batten, but that would mean missing out on the walk across the River Plym on Laira Bridge. The depot is no longer there; a relief road has been cut through part of the site but the rest remains undeveloped. At the far end of the bridge it is possible to see the Chelson Meadow premises, built for First but now occupied by Stagecoach South West. The stop at which Bristol FLF6G/ECW 2054 (BUO 202B) is waiting was used for crew changeovers; it has come from Elburton and will cross the city centre on its way to the Torpoint ferry. The side advertisement on 2054 referring to the 'big fuel saver' may be a reference to the shortages that occurred in 1974. Other reminders of that bygone age are the parcels service notice – a practice that continued into the 1980s – and the Midland Bank logo on the bus shelter; it would be another twenty-five years before it was phased out completely under HSBC management.

ON SUNDAY, 5 SEPTEMBER 1999, Western National held the 'New Era' rally as a farewell to its Laira Bridge depot, and this gathering at the main gates is of current and former staff. My thanks to the then Business Development Manager, Vicki Cheetham (front row, in the white t-shirt), for letting me have a copy of the photograph. The VR3 is 1203 (LFJ 847W), one of two given a special livery to mark the seventieth anniversary of

Laira Bridge pictured in 1997.

Western National, the other being Camborne resident 1141 for services in Cornwall. Laira Bridge had been home to Western National since 1929, and had been largely rebuilt after suffering two devastating strikes by the Luftwaffe during the Second World War. The new depot, on the opposite bank of the River Plym at The Ride, Chelson Meadow, was officially opened later that month.

THERE IS A marvellous view of Plymouth and the Tamar estuary from Jennycliff, and in 2019 it was served by Target Travel 54, which was extended to Bovisand. This was also the case in 1997 when it was Western National 17, a summer service advertised as an open-top bus operation. So on a warm, sunny day, 27 July, I set out to photograph it, assuming it would be Laira Bridge's resident open-top VR, 944, performing the honours. But 944 was nowhere to be seen, and its somewhat underwhelming (and sparsely patronised) replacement was 1200 (LFJ 844W), one of the VR3s normally found on the opposite side of Plymouth, since it had been converted for use on the Torpoint ferry.

7

Plymouth (Jennycliffe Bay) to Paignton: 73 Miles

Total so far: 492 miles

On this section

From Jennycliff, the Path heads past a number of small, and in some cases, exclusive, holiday locations – Bigbury-on-Sea and Burgh Island, Bantham, and Hope Cove – before arriving at Salcombe. From here it is a short distance to Start Point, where the route now heads north-east to Dartmouth and Brixham. This section ends at Paignton, by which time we have almost reached the heart of Torbay. There are five stretches of water that must be negotiated: the rivers Yealm, Erne, Avon and Dart, and the Kingsbridge estuary. Sometimes a detour inland is needed. Ferry crossings are required at Wembury, Salcombe and Dartmouth.

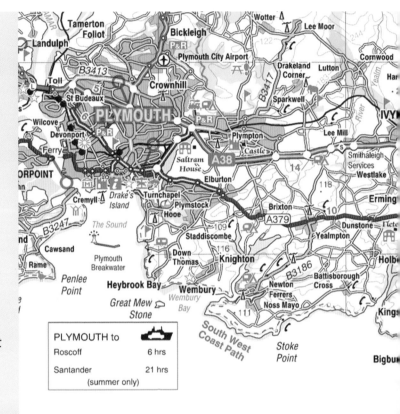

PLYMOUTH to	🚢
Roscoff	6 hrs
Santander	21 hrs
(summer only)	

Burgh Island at low tide.

Paignton Pier.

Things to see

This is beyond doubt the busiest section we have encountered thus far. Salcombe, though small, is a bustling resort and gives easy access to sandy beaches; each year there is both a town and Yacht Club Regatta. The Torcross and Slapton Sands area was requisitioned in 1943 as a practice area for the D-Day landings; the exercise did not go according to plan, and hundreds of US lives were lost as a result. A Sherman tank was recovered from the sea in 1994, and now stands in the main car park. Slapton Ley is the largest freshwater lake in south-west England, and is the site of a National Nature Reserve. Dartmouth has hosted the annual

The bustling resort of Salcombe.

(Adobe Stoc

A view of Torcross and Slapton Sands, the practice area for the D-Day landings.
(Paul Wilkinson)

The recovered Sherman tank stands in the main carpark behind the houses.

Royal Regatta since 1822, and has many buildings of historical significance, including the Royal Castle Hotel and the Butterwalk, both dating from the 1630s. Although now in use as a restaurant, the building on the river side of the North Embankment was originally Dartmouth station, although there was never a railway line here; passengers arrived at Kingswear, on the opposite bank of the Dart, and were conveyed to Dartmouth by ferry. Kingswear station is now the southern terminus for the heritage Dartmouth Steam Railway. Brixham is the smallest of the three towns that

The inner harbour at Dartmouth looking across the river towards Kingswear.

Paignton beach.

make up the unitary authority of Torbay. Tourism and fishing are the main occupations; there is a replica of the *Golden Hind*, Sir Francis Drake's ship, moored there. Finally Paignton, the northern terminus of the heritage line and now the end of the line for GWR services from Paddington via Torquay. Principally a seaside resort, with several excellent beaches, it also boasts a fine pier and a famous zoo.

An outline of services past...

Historically, coastal destinations between Plymouth and Dartmouth were served by Great Western Railway bus services, along with a host of small independents that were, in the main, bought out after Western National came on the scene in 1929. Devon General was founded in May 1919, but was taken over by the Torquay Tramways Company three years later. However, the directors resolved to trade under the Devon General name, and this situation lasted until 1996, despite the company being merged with Western National in NBC days from the start of 1971 to the end of 1982. The Stagecoach group took over in 1996.

...and present

Routes that follow the course of the Path between Plymouth and Salcombe are limited: Tally Ho Coaches service 94 links Plymouth with Noss Mayo and Newton Ferrers, and their 875 comprises one return journey on weekdays to Bigbury-on-Sea. Tally Ho also operates service 162 (Kingsbridge, Thurlestone and Hope Cove circular) and 606 (Kingsbridge–Salcombe; 164 on Sundays). But principal routes, which are provided by Stagecoach South West, follow the main A379:

- service 3 links Plymouth with Kingsbridge and Dartmouth. It is only the section from Torcross to Dartmouth that is as true as can be to the Path
- take the Lower Ferry or Passenger Ferry to Kingswear
- service 18 links Kingswear and Brixham
- service Hop 12 links Brixham and Paignton

GWR 912 (XY 2104), a Thorneycroft A1 with Vickers B19F bodywork new in 1925, in an evocative postcard view at Bigbury-on-Sea when still quite youthful. It passed to Western National in 1929, retaining the same fleet number, at which point the route from Plymouth became the 92. This was an early casualty of the NBC era, though by the end of the 1970s, the 99 offered four return journeys on Sundays and Bank Holidays during the holiday season. In 2019, the route now operates to and from Plymouth as Tally Ho 875.

BURGH ISLAND LIES around 300 yards off the coast at Bigbury-on-Sea. When the tide is out, visitors can walk across the sand to see the Pilchard Inn, built in 1336, or the luxury, art deco-styled Burgh Island Hotel, which in its time has played host to Agatha Christie; Noel Coward; Edward VIII and Mrs Simpson; Winston Churchill, and the Beatles, to name just a few. But on all other occasions, be prepared for a most unusual ride aboard the hotel's sea tractor! The current vehicle is the third to have been used; it was built in 1969, and crossings cost £2 each way. A maximum of thirty passengers can be carried in the daytime, reducing to twenty after dark. There is a warning not to touch the machinery or obstruct the driver, whose authority is 'final at all times', according to the rules board. High tide was still a couple of hours away on 22 May 2018, but already the sea is half-covering the wheels. It may only travel at 5mph, and the crossing last no longer than 5 minutes, but riding aboard the sea tractor, variously described as iconic and unique, is an unforgettable experience.

THE GREAT WESTERN Railway branch line from South Brent to Kingsbridge opened in December 1893. For the first fifteen years, stagecoaches took holidaymakers on to Salcombe, but the GWR began to operate buses between Kingsbridge and Salcombe from July 1909 – its first route in the area. By 1911 it had been extended to Modbury, and from 1921, a through service to Dartmouth was established. When Western National was formed in 1929, the Salcombe service became the 105. The terminus has always been on Shadycombe Road (where Western National inherited a small garage from the GWR), some way from the centre, but as anyone who has visited Salcombe will know, the narrow roads are not particularly bus-friendly, especially in summer. Tally Ho Coaches have had the main Monday–Saturday route, the 606, for many years now, and also operate a summer park-and-ride service which does get to within a stone's throw of the sea. Not everyone that we can see waiting in Market Street for Optare Solo YJ55 YHG will manage to get a ride; fortunately, the next one was not far behind.

AT THIS POINT it is necessary to deviate from the route of the Path to look at a short-lived initiative designed to assist walkers in the South Hams area. The Coast Path Hopper Bus was introduced in 1998, offering two services every Saturday and Sunday between 16 May and 19 July; daily from 23 July to 31 August; and on Saturdays and Sundays again between 5 and 27 September. It consisted of two circular services:

> • 158 'Western loop' (Kingsbridge–Salcombe–Inner Hope–Thurlestone–Kingsbridge), at 09:15 (clockwise) and 14:00 (anti-clockwise), journey time 1 hour 50 minutes
> • 159 'Eastern loop' (Kingsbridge–Chillington–Beesands–Start Point–East Portlemouth–South Pool–Kingsbridge), at 11:15 (anti-clockwise) and 16:00 (clockwise), journey time 1 hour 48 minutes

The Hopper was linked to a baggage service, the South West Coast Path Packhorse, which covered the coast from Fowey to Beesands. Walkers could drop off their bags at any depot in the morning, and they would be ready for collection at the depot of their choice in the afternoon.

Mercedes L608D 113 (C956 GAF) was photographed in South Pool on 14 August 1998. Despite the fact that the routes were highly commended in the Bus Industry Awards that year, unfortunately they were not a great success; in 1999, the 158 was dropped but the 159 was increased to two trips in either direction, operating daily from 30 May to 25 September. In 2000, no longer advertised as the Coast Path Hopper, it fell to three services a day, and in 2001, it was withdrawn.

THE FORMER FISHING village of Torcross lies at the point where the A379 turns to the coast on its way to Dartmouth, and in 2012, the Olympic torch relay, which began at Land's End, called there on the second day, 20 May, on the leg from Plymouth to Exeter. The procession included a Wright Streetlite, ten of which were temporarily diverted from a Stagecoach South Wales order, whose function was to transport the torchbearers, and a coach for other personnel. Two of these were supplied by Buzzlines Travel of Hythe, and this is BT08 BUZ, a Van Hool Alicron new to Cronin, Cork. All wore the dedicated orange and white livery.
(Deborah Bartlett)

THE 93 DARTMOUTH–PLYMOUTH route was upgraded in April 2007 when four ex-London Dennis Trident/Plaxton Presidents were allocated to it. They arrived from London the year before for temporary use on Plymouth Park & Ride services, but after conversion to single door and a repaint into a rather fetching green, cream and blue livery they were ready to operate what was now marketed as the 'Mayflower Link'. They were themselves replaced in 2010 by four more ex-Centrewest Tridents, one of which, 33174 (LR02 LYT) was seen in Torcross on 21 September 2012.

TALLY HO VOLVO B10M/PLAXTON C195 CYO, seen returning to Kingsbridge after an afternoon school run in September 2012, on the A379 just outside Torcross. The South West Coast Path is on the right of the picture.

SOUTH-EASTERLY WINDS and storm conditions can wreak havoc with the coastline between Torcross and Strete Gate. In 2001, the A379 was closed for several months after a section of road collapsed, and the same happened again in early March 2018, when Storm Emma met 'the beast from the east', and once again a lengthy closure occurred. As happened on the previous occasion, the bus service, by now the 3 and operated by Stagecoach South West, was diverted at Strete along a narrow country lane to the A3122 and the A381 directly to Kingsbridge, while a shuttle bus operated from Kingsbridge to Slapton Memorial, where this photo was taken on 25 May 2018. ADL Enviro 200 37142 (YY14 WGZ) will shortly reverse into Sands Road, and set off back towards Torcross.

IN 2004, FIRST Devon & Cornwall introduced an open-top service between Dartmouth and Kingsbridge. Marketed as the 'Primrose Explorer' and numbered 393, to distinguish it from the main route, it carried a flat fare of £5.50. Ex-Aberdeen Leyland Atlantean/Alexander 39903 (HRS 271V) was the chosen vehicle, and on 20 June, with the broad sweep of the English Channel in the background, it was making the steep climb out of Blackpool Sands towards Strete. The route was not a success and was withdrawn at the end of its first season.

THE DARTMOUTH PARK & Ride contract was in the hands of Tally Ho! Coaches of Kingsbridge in 2007, and as this photo shows, it was hard-pressed to cope with the extra crowds that converge on the town for the annual Royal Regatta. Dennis Dart/Wright Handybus J616 KCU was one of the larger vehicles being used that day (31 August) and it had taken my group 40 minutes to get from the top of the temporary site to the front of the queue. However, that was nothing compared to a wait of 90 minutes on the return journey.

Incidentally, the '!' in the Tally Ho! company name was dropped after a change of ownership in 2008.

THE PATH BRINGS us to Dartmouth via Blackpool Sands and Stoke Fleming, and en route to the centre of the town stands the castle, which has guarded the strategically important port since the late fourteenth century. The inner harbour, or boat float, lies at the heart of the town, and it is there that we see a vehicle belonging to the Dartmouth & District Bus Company. Founded in 1929, it operated services to Dittisham and to Cornworthy and Ashprington. In 1934, with Western National seeking depot facilities in the town, the premises in Mayor's Avenue and three vehicles were acquired. A new depot was opened on the site in 1936, and the Dittisham route became the 144, while Cornworthy was the 107. The three buses were numbered 3493–95; respectively a Morris B14, a Laffley B24, and a Willeys Knight fourteen-seater coach with Mumford bodywork; this would appear to be the Laffley, pictured prior to the change of ownership.

I am very grateful to Mr C King of Falmouth for making the print, taken from a 3¼in. lantern slide, available to me.

BRISTOL FLF6G 1973 (472 FTT), new in January 1961, spent much of its life in Cornwall but in the summer of 1981 put in an appearance at Dartmouth, specifically, it would seem, for park-and-ride duty. Despite the fact that the vehicle is 20 years old and there is no route number or destination display, the relevant information is carried in the area normally reserved for advertisements, which is arguably as eye-catching. With sixty-eight seats, it would certainly have been more effective at crowd-moving than the Tally Ho! Dennis Dart seen earlier. After its stint in the sun, 1973 was despatched to Bideford, but was withdrawn in March 1982.

AS IT SEEMS to feature on almost every Devonian day tour itinerary, Dartmouth sees a huge amount of coach traffic. On 27 May 2010, there were six coaches lined up along the North Embankment, four of them in Shearings National Holidays' livery. At the head of affairs was 559 (YJ03 VMT), a Transbus (Plaxton)-bodied Volvo B10M new to Wallace Arnold. Service buses – which at this time served Townstal (90), Kingsbridge and Plymouth (93), Torquay (X81) and the unnumbered Park & Ride – used the parking spaces closer to the former railway station turned restaurant, but it could sometimes be a tight squeeze.

THE DART ESTUARY is crossed by way of one of three ferries, known as the 'Higher', 'Lower' and 'Passenger'. The Lower Ferry is the smallest of the three, and operates from slipways in the centre of Dartmouth and Kingswear. It provides a more direct link to the continuation of the Path. The Higher Ferry, pictured here, also known as the 'Floating Bridge', can accommodate thirty-six vehicles, and was introduced into service in 2009, although there has been a ferry here since the 1830s. Walkers using this ferry need to follow the footpath alongside the Dartmouth Steam Railway to get to Kingswear. The Passenger Ferry leaves Dartmouth from the waterfront, adjacent to the former station building, and docks on the opposite side at the steam railway terminus.

THE DARTMOUTH STEAM Railway, formerly the Paignton & Dartmouth Steam Railway, began its life as a heritage line in 1973, after it was sold by British Railways to the Dart Valley Light Railway Ltd. The principal operating season is usually between April and October; there is low season running in all other months, bar January. Leaving Kingswear for Paignton and seen close to the Higher Ferry crossing in August 2002, was Swindon-built Great Western 2-8-0T 5239 Goliath. It is still part of the company's rolling stock, though at the time of writing it was being overhauled at the East Somerset Railway.

BEFORE 1960, BUSES on the Brixham–Kingswear service, jointly operated by Devon General and Burton's Cars of Brixham, had a difficult manoeuvre to perform upon reaching the Lower Ferry departure point in Kingswear. Burton's all Leyland PD2/10 POD 100 was adapted so that it would fit under the arch of the Royal Dart Hotel, after which it would reverse back towards the cars waiting for the ferry, which is what the policeman is keeping a helpful eye on! In 1960, a turning circle was built overlooking the railway, further up the road, thus ending a tradition of low-bridge double deckers from both companies on the route.

HAVING NOW CROSSED the River Dart to Kingswear, we come to a bus stand built so that it juts out above the railway, supported on huge concrete pillars. Built in 1960, it was quickly christened the 'Banjo' due to its shape, and the name has stuck ever since. Saturday, 31 August 2002 was the last day of that year's Royal Regatta at Dartmouth, and providing some extra capacity, though with few takers, was Duchy Travel's Bristol VR3/ECW MOU 739R. The 12D was in direct competition with four different routes operated by Stagecoach across the Torbay area. The vehicle was new to Bristol (5065), passing later to Cheltenham & Gloucester and arriving in Devon in 2000. It was sold on to a Winchester company in 2003, the same year that Duchy Travel went into liquidation.

THE TORBAY AREA saw the introduction of large numbers of minibuses early in 1986. Of the fifty-one Ford Transits delivered at that time, all bar four entered service in a new dark red and ivory livery with Bayline fleetnames. The first seventeen were bodied by Robin Hood, the remainder, including 511 (C511 FFJ) by Carlyle, and it is to be hoped that its sixteen seats will be sufficient to carry all the intending passengers, in this view taken at The Strand, Brixham, on 3 July 1986. The replica Golden Hind is visible in the background.

THE 12 IS ANOTHER Devonian service with a long history. Originally a Torquay Tramways bus route between Paignton and Brixham, it gained its number in 1922. It was extended to Torquay by 1928 and to Newton Abbot in June 1953. It was a bastion of Devon General's minibus operations, but after Devon General was acquired by the Stagecoach group, larger vehicles were soon reintroduced. One such was 929 (J829 HMC), a Scania N113DRB/Alexander RH which was new to London Buses (S29) and subsequently Stagecoach East London, where it had formed part of the Docklands Express fleet. It came to Devon in 2000, and on this occasion – 8 June 2001 – it was heading out of Market Street, Brixham. It seems safe to assume that its final destination will be Newton Abbot, although there clearly is an issue with the blinds. It would later be converted to open-top format, and was not withdrawn until the end of the 2013 season.

DEVON GENERAL INTRODUCED open-top double deckers for the first time in 1955, the vehicles selected being six AEC Regents new in 1934/35. They lasted until 1961, when the 'Sea Dog' Atlanteans were acquired. The next development came in 1976, when AEC Regent Vs 507 and 508 were converted to operate a new service between Torquay and Dawlish Warren. This is 507 Prince Regent (507 RUO), having a spot of bother in Paignton bus station whilst working the more intensive seafront service to Torquay. The livery – poppy red and white with a red band – was subsequently applied to the new VR3 'Warship' class when they arrived in 1978, at which point the Regent Vs were withdrawn and sold for further use in London with the Obsolete Fleet operation.

THE NEW KID on the Torbay open-top bus scene has been Dart Pleasure Craft Ltd, trading as 'Rail River Link'. It is owned by the company that operates the Dartmouth Steam Railway, the passenger ferry between Dartmouth and Kingswear, and other craft used for river and coastal cruises. It entered the bus market in 2000 with a Totnes–Paignton service (which mirrored First Western National's X80), using two open-top VR3s from Stagecoach Devon, whose former 937 became 1 (UWV 614S) in its new guise. Seen leaving Paignton bus station on 29 May 2013, Frankie survived for a further three years before withdrawal.

8

Paignton to Seaton: 45 Miles

Total so far: 537 miles

On this section

The Path leaves Paignton by the Esplanade and Torbay Road on its way to Torquay, the heart of the 'English Riviera', and Babbacombe. At Shaldon, a ferry will take passengers across the estuary to Teignmouth, although excellent views can also be had by temporarily leaving the Path to cross by the road bridge. The section between Teignmouth and Dawlish Warren follows the railway for the most part. At Dawlish, the works that have been carried out after the storms of 2014 can be seen. When really high tides and bad weather contrive to make parts of this walk difficult or impassable, recourse to the A379 is required. Following the road past Cockwood brings us to Starcross and another ferry crossing will land us in Exmouth, but this only operates between April and October. Otherwise the best options are the buses or trains from Starcross to Exeter, and Exeter to Exmouth. But now we have reached the Jurassic Coast, a World Heritage Site since 2001, which will be with us for most of the rest of our journey. First, there are four traditional English resorts, Budleigh Salterton, Sidmouth, Beer and Seaton, which lie between Exmouth and the Devon county border. Progress along the Path until just west of Sidmouth is relatively straightforward, but subsequently, there are steep climbs and descents, and diversions put in place after storms in the 2010s.

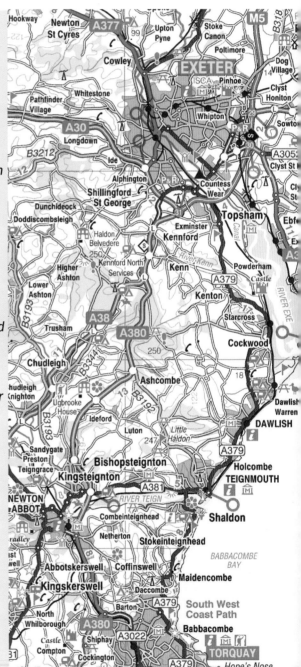

Things to see

Amongst Torquay's many attractions is Kents Cavern, a series of prehistoric caves that for many years were advertised on almost every Devon General and Western National bus! Babbacombe is home to the famous model village, and where the cliff railway has

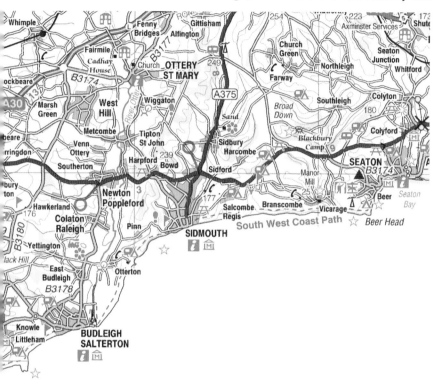

Torquay harbour.

been taking sun worshippers down to Oddicombe Beach almost continually since it opened in 1926.

Whilst in Seaton, a ride on the tramway is essential. This 3-mile narrow-gauge route from Colyton utilises part of the Seaton branch line, which closed in 1966, the trams arriving four years later. No. 12, seen above, was photographed at Colyton in 2001.

At Starcross, the former pumping engine house, pictured left, is now used by a sailing club but was originally part of Brunel's clever, though flawed, plan for an atmospheric railway between Exeter and Newton Abbot. A combination of the line's close relationship with the sea, and the rodents that took a liking to the leather flaps that sealed the vacuum pipes, meant the system operated for under a year.

An outline of bus services past...

Devon General was the dominant operator from the 1920s through to 1996, and Stagecoach South West has since assumed that role. Even when Devon General was administered by Western National, for the most part it retained its own fleetname and NBC red livery. North Devon (Red Bus) linked Sidmouth with Lyme Regis on Sundays until 2000, and a number of small independents operated tendered services for Devon County Council – and still do.

...and present

Looking at the bus services on this section of the Path, only two are required to take us up to the River Exe estuary:

- service 22 links Paignton with Torquay, Babbacombe, Shaldon, Teignmouth, Dawlish and Dawlish Warren
- service 2 omits Dawlish Warren, but links Dawlish with Starcross

At Starcross, take the ferry to Exmouth, then:

- service 95 links Exmouth and Sandy Bay
- service 157 links Exmouth and Budleigh Salterton with Sidmouth
- service 899 links Sidmouth, Beer and Seaton

The 885 also works between Beer and Seaton. All are operated by Stagecoach South West apart from the 885/899, which are provided by Axe Valley Mini Travel, based in Seaton.

AMONG THE LAST vehicles to be delivered to Devon General before it was subsumed within Western National on 1 January 1971 were eight AEC Reliance/Willowbrook B43F saloons. None of them entered service before this event took place. 80 (TUO 80J) was seen in Torbay Road, Torquay, on a short working of the 149 to the Broadpark Estate. The class received NBC livery in the mid-1970s; some had the white band extended under the windscreen, thus making it difficult to carry advertisements there. They were all withdrawn in 1980.

ONE OF THE nine legendary Devon General 'Sea Dogs', Leyland Atlantean/MCCW convertible open-top 926 Sir Francis Drake (926 GTA), seen on 22 July 1964 in Vaughan Road, Torquay, outside the Pavilion. The reversed ivory and red livery looks superb.

BY 1998, DEVON General's open-top fleet was down to three. Enter 992 (LRV 992), a Weymann-bodied Leyland PD2/12, new in 1956 to Portsmouth and which, along with five of its sisters, had

lost its roof at least twenty years earlier. It came to Torquay in November 1997 from Thames Transit, and after some use as a tree-lopper, was given Stagecoach corporate livery and put to work between Paignton and Torquay. I found it in Babbacombe Road, Torquay on 22 June 2000, after a repaint into the more becoming ivory and red scheme. When the national numbering system was introduced, it became 19992, and in 2019 it still forms part of the South West fleet – a 'special' special events vehicle approaching its 65th birthday.

AN EARLY SUMMER haze settles on the fields above the villages of Shaldon and Ringmore as Stagecoach South West 15868 (WA62 AOM) crosses the River Teign by way of Shaldon Bridge on 23 May 2018. It has come from Paignton on the lengthy 22. The photo was taken from a vantage point close to the junction of the A379 (which you see here) with the A381, giving a perfect, uninterrupted view of the bridge.

FIVE BRISTOL RELL6Gs, 225-29, delivered in 1973, were the first buses to be allocated to Devon General in NBC livery. They were dual door examples, a format latterly favoured by City of Exeter. 225 (ATA 225L) went briefly to Western National in 1982 for conversion to DP21D, to allow use by disabled passengers. Duly restored to Devon General and in this special livery, it was seen at the Triangle, Teignmouth in August 1985.

AS THIS POSTCARD view shows, the Great Western main line separates the seaside town of Dawlish from the sea. Not an issue when the weather is fine, but like many places along this stretch of coast, problems are quick to arise when easterly winds and high seas combine. In 1974, part of the down platform at the station was lost, and the storms of January 2014 destroyed the sea wall and washed away part of the line, leaving the rails hanging in mid-air, on the stretch we can see here. However, all is calm in what appears to be a summertime post-war photo, which also includes two Devon General saloons. Nearest the camera is SR458 (DOD 458), a 1940 AEC Regal/Weymann which was rebodied by Portsmouth Aviation in 1948. Often found on the 2 (Exeter–Newton Abbot), it was fitted with a canvas roof when new, and would regularly run with it open, apparently at all times of the year. This feature was, however, lost upon overhaul.

PUTTING GREEN DAWLISH. 22052.

CAFES AND ARCADES line Richmond Place, opposite the railway station, where Dartline's Optare Solo YJ16 DFC is waiting time before departing for Sainsbury's. The 186 originally linked Exeter and Dawlish; it was cut back to work Starcross–Dawlish, until its current incarnation as the Dawlish town service. Dartline Coaches was founded in 1987 and has a sizeable coach tours programme and local bus portfolio that reaches as far north as Taunton.

(Photo courtesy of the
NHVC Collection)

TWO PHOTOGRAPHS, TAKEN from an identical position in Beach
Road, Dawlish Warren, but separated in time by around fifty years.
In the one above, Devon General 886 (886 ATA), a Leyland
Atlantean with Metro Cammell bodywork, one of seventeen new
in 1959, has arrived from Torquay with a 13 working. This was
originally a Torquay Tramways service to Shaldon, extended
progressively to Teignmouth, then Dawlish, until it came to Dawlish
Warren (in the summer only) in 1963. But this
looks to be a few years later, judging by the young
lady's miniskirt. Showing off the red and ivory
livery to the very best advantage, 886 remained
with Devon General for all its twenty-two year
service life.

THIS WAS THE scene in Beach Road on 23 May
2018, with Stagecoach South West 15860 (WA62
AKU) newly arrived from Paignton. When 'Hop'
branding was originally introduced, the route
was the 11, from Torquay. Change came in the
summer of 2016, when it gained the number 22,
starting back from South Devon College, just
outside Paignton. Total journey time in 2019 is a
little over 2 hours.

WE HAVE NOW crossed the River Exe and arrived in Exmouth. Devon General first opened a depot here in 1921, but a new garage was built ten years later. This lasted until 1980, when it was demolished, leaving just a bus station and service area. Finally in 2016, the area was cleared and is now a Marks & Spencer store. On 18 August 1985, dual door Leyland National 232 (GFJ 660N) was standing, out of service, in the yard.

THIS IS THE TRIANGLE in Sidmouth, which serves as a pick-up point as well as a terminus for the town's bus services. The principal routes are Stagecoach South West's 9/9A from Exeter to Honiton (9) or Lyme Regis (9A), but local operator Axe Valley Mini Travel provides useful links to Beer and Seaton. I went along on 26 September 2012 to sample the 899, and was met by a rainstorm of what seemed to be approaching biblical proportions. A conveniently close shelter allowed me to stay relatively dry and get a photo of P503 RYM, a Dennis Dart SLF/ Plaxton Pointer which was new in 1996 to London General (LDP3) and had joined the fleet in 2011. It has since been withdrawn.

Seaton to South Haven Point: 45 Miles

Total so far: 630 miles

On this section

The Path continues through the heart of the Jurassic Coast, but walkers beware! There have been many cliff falls, particularly between Lyme Regis and beyond West Bay. There is a Jurassic Park Heritage Centre at Charmouth. Golden Cap, at 627ft (191 metres) is the highest point on the south coast of England. Chesil Beach is an 18-mile shingle bank which stretches all the way from West Bay to Portland; it is possible to walk along it from Abbotsbury to Wyke Regis. The Path goes right round Portland, an 'almost island', en route to Weymouth, after which some spectacular coastal scenery greets us as we pass Durdle Door and Lulworth Cove. The Path passes the Lulworth army firing ranges, which means it may be closed at certain times for obvious reasons! There are excellent views to be had from St Aldhelm's Head. After the resort of Swanage, the rocks of Old Harry are popular with photographers. The last part of the Path is at sea level, and passes the naturist part of Studland Beach – there is an avoiding route – before finishing at South Haven Point.

Things to see

Starting in Lyme Regis, this picturesque, though hilly, resort is probably best known for its harbour and sea wall, the Cobb, and which for the most part date from the 1820s. They feature in both Persuasion (Jane Austen), where Louisa Musgrove jumps off the steps, known as 'Granny's Teeth', and is concussed, and *The French Lieutenant's Woman*. In the film, Meryl Streep – or perhaps a stunt double – walks amidst the rain and spray from the sea to the end of the wall. The TV drama *Broadchurch* was filmed at West Bay, which also has a 200-year old ship's cannon mounted at

A late evening view of Chesil Beach taken in June 2019 from the hill above Fortuneswell. The gathering gloom lends a mysterious air to the scene.

The Cobb at Lyme Regis, photographed in 2002.

Lulworth Cove.

Durdle Door near Lulworth Cove.

Steam train at Swanage railway station.

the end of the old West Pier. Portland boasts one of the largest man-made harbours in the world, and quarrying of the local stone (which graces part of Buckingham Palace, St Paul's Cathedral and the Cenotaph) has taken place since at least the 1600s. Portland Castle, dating from a century earlier, is managed by English Heritage and open to the public. The earliest railway here was opened in 1826; the last trains ran in April 1965. Weymouth has a revolving viewing tower known as the Jurassic Skyline, a Sealife

Park, and Sandworld, where visitors can build their own creations. The Weymouth Harbour Line was, until its closure in 1987, used to bring passengers to and from the ferries to the main station. Part of the route involved street running, and the lines are still extant. Durdle Door and Lulworth Cove both provide stunning coastal scenery. Swanage also has a connection with the railway, and despite the fact that it was severed from the main line at Wareham in 1972, reopening has taken place in stages since 1979. The first through running from London Victoria took place in 2009, and regular passenger services to Wareham began in 2017.

An outline of bus services past...

Lyme Regis was first reached by Devon General in 1923; it marked the easternmost extent of their day-to-day operations; from there to Swanage was largely in the hands of Southern National. Despite being called Wilts & Dorset, that company, founded in 1915, was to be found mainly in southern Wiltshire and northern Hampshire. It was merged with Hants & Dorset in 1972, but was reborn in 1983. Its area was expanded to include operations from Swanage to Poole and Bournemouth.

...and present

• Stagecoach South West service 9A links Seaton and Lyme Regis
• First Wessex Dorset & South Somerset X53 – the Jurassic Coaster – links Lyme Regis with Charmouth, West Bay, Abbotsbury and Weymouth
• The same company's service 1 links Weymouth and Southwell on the Isle of Portland. In summer, service 501 continues to Portland Bill. Return to Weymouth
• Their service X54 links Weymouth with Lulworth Cove and Wareham. In summer, Go South Coast Breezer 30 links Lulworth Cove with Swanage; otherwise the same company's 40 links Wareham and Swanage
• Go South Coast 50/Breezer 50 links Swanage and Shell Bay

FOR A TIME in the 1990s, North Devon (Red Bus) had a presence a long way from its Exeter outstation, with the Sundays and Bank Holidays 378, which linked Lyme Regis (just inside the Dorset border) with Sidmouth. Waiting in Broad Street, Lyme Regis on 18 June 2000, with the English Channel shimmering in the background, was Wright-bodied Mercedes 811D 6371 (K752 XTA). Following the end of operations at Exeter later that year, the 378 passed to Stagecoach Devon.

LEYLAND NATIONAL 2850 (PTT 90R) was a Weymouth vehicle from new, and as such passed to Southern National on 1 January 1983, where it soldiered on until withdrawal, at the age of 22 – an excellent age for the type – in November 1998. Negotiating Bridge Street in Lyme Regis, as 2850 is doing here, would have been interesting at peak holiday times. It was bound for Taunton in 1986 – a journey that cannot be undertaken today without at least one change – but the Lyme Fossil Shop, which can be seen in the background, is still going strong today.

A TRIP TO West Bay on 18 June 2019 suffered because of mist and drizzle, and the resort itself was undergoing some major sea defences work. Into all this came First Wessex, Dorset & South Somerset 37998 (BF63 HDX), a Volvo B9TL/Wrightbus Eclipse Gemini 2 in the latest Jurassic Coaster livery of yellow and red. Despite the weather, it still had a healthy loading. There have been many route variations over the years since it was introduced in 2002, when one could travel from Exeter to Poole without a change. Nowadays, it has been cut back at the western end to Axminster; the X53 goes from there to Weymouth, and the X54 from Weymouth to Poole. A third service, the X51, links Axminster and Dorchester.

PORTLAND HAS BEEN described as an 'almost island', as it is linked to the mainland only by the southern end of Chesil Beach. Outside of the peak season, buses venture only as far as Southwell, where on 31 March 1993 I found Southern National 711 (J140 SJT), a Mercedes 709D/Wright – new the previous year. It was later reallocated to Barnstaple, so was with North Devon (Red Bus) and thus subsumed by Western National in 1999, taking the new fleet number 6520.

PORTLAND BILL LIGHTHOUSE lies a further 1½ miles from Southwell. It has been in use since 1906, though the Old Higher and Old Lower lighthouses have a history going back to 1716. The buildings they occupied between 1869 and 1906 still stand, and are Grade II listed.

IT IS PERHAPS not widely known that the Great Western Railway began sailings from Weymouth to the Channel Islands and French ports as early as 1889. In 1948, the shipping fleets owned by the former railway companies, LMS, LNER, SR and GWR, were brought together under British Railways control. The name Sealink was introduced in 1968, becoming a separate company – Sealink UK Ltd – in May 1979. At the same time, Western National decked out its Bristol FLF6G 2080 (BDV 259C) in appropriate advertising, its new task being to transport passengers, with all their attendant baggage, to and from the ferries. It lasted in this guise until the end of 1980, and was replaced by Leyland National 2823, which in due course also received the Sealink livery.

SOUTHERN NATIONAL ACQUIRED two of the eleven Western National open-top VR3s (934 and 942) in 1983. It added a third in 1985, but the work was carried out in-house and unlike the others, 555 (ATA 555L) was not capable of being re-roofed. Named 'Sir Christopher Wren', it received this attractive green and cream livery and a fake Bristol plate. It was to be found on Weymouth's Esplanade, or King's Statue as it appeared in timetables, bound for Bowleaze Cove, north-east of the resort, on 24 August 1986.

ON THE SAME day that I saw Southern National 555, I also visited Lulworth Cove. It appears that Grandma and the boys may have arrived here aboard Shamrock & Rambler 132 (YOY 132, JDG 285V), a Duple-bodied Leyland Leopard, which in common with the rest of the fleet had been named, in this case, Hawk. Based in Bournemouth, the company was formed in 1924 by a merger of the two operators, Shamrock and Rambler, which were then absorbed into Hants & Dorset in NBC days. The name reappeared in 1983 in consequence of another pre-privatisation split. A foray into the world of minibuses proved unsuccessful, and following acquisition by the Drawlane group in in 1987, the loss of National Express contracts in April 1989 led to Shamrock & Rambler's demise.

A BRIEF HISTORY of Wilts & Dorset was recounted earlier, but to bring matters up to date, it was sold to the Go-Ahead group in 2003. The service between Swanage and Bournemouth is now the 50, and is colourfully marketed under the 'Purbeck Breezer' name. Newly arrived at Swanage station on 17 June 2019, 1706 (HJ16 HTC) is a partial open-top Volvo B5TL with MCV Evoseti bodywork.

WILTS & DORSET devised this attractive red, white and black livery in 1987, the year of its management buyout from NBC. When North Devon (Red Bus) parted with its two ECW-bodied Leyland Olympians in 1986, both only 2 years old, Wilts & Dorset took them and rebuilt them as convertible open-toppers. Their suspension was adjusted to allow them to use the Shell Bay to Sandbanks chain ferry, the first double deckers ever to do so. 3907 (A990 XAF) has come from Bournemouth on 16 August 1987, and is fully laden.

We have now reached the end of the South West Coast Path.

BUT JUST AS we began the journey a couple of miles before the start of the Path, let us finish it by going on a little further. Before the Leyland Olympians came on the scene, the 150 played host to forty-three-seater Bristol LH6Ls, ten of which by the time of this photo – August 1986 – had been modified by shortening their front panels, allowing them to use the ferry. Here we see 3854 (AFB 590B) at the front of the queue at Shell Bay. As more Olympians arrived, the LHs spent less time on the ferry, but some continued to give good service up to the end of the 1990s.

LEAVING THE FERRY, we reach the appropriately named Panorama Road in Sandbanks. Bournemouth Transport had for many years used the fleetname Yellow Buses, as displayed on Alexander-bodied Daimler Fleetline 133 (NFX 133P). One of eight new in 1976, which were convertible to open-top (three more were added in 1978), it was working the 11 to Christchurch Quay on 30 August 1986. Part of the RATP group prior to a management buyout in July 2019, Yellow Buses still operate an open-top service in summer, now known as 'Buster's Beach Bus'.

But let us return to the Shell Bay side of the ferry, or South Haven Point as it is properly known, to officially close this journey along the South West Coast Path. This is the impressive steel sculpture that marks the end, which stands just a matter of yards from the bus stop seen in the photo of the open-top Wilts & Dorset decker.

Those who braved the Path on foot will have amassed some fairly amazing statistics:

• they will have walked a total of 630.2 miles, or 1,014.2 kilometres over the entire distance

• they will have climbed a total of 114,907ft (35,024 metres): that is almost four times the height of Mount Everest. Presumably they will have descended around the same amount; about three times more than the deepest part of the Mariana Trench in the Pacific Ocean!

• they may have used over twenty ferry crossings, and according

to a survey taken some years ago, passed 2,473 signposts or waymarks, crossed 302 bridges and 921 stiles, and negotiated 26,719 steps

• they will have contributed around £500 million to the local economy

The South West Coast Path
near Lynmouth.

Those who have tried to follow the Path by bus will have travelled well in excess of 630 miles. As of 2019, they would have used fourteen different operators, eight of them independents.

The South West Coast Path is to be incorporated into a new national trail, to be known as the England Coast Path, which is expected to be completed in 2020 (a Wales Coast Path opened in 2012), making yet more of our beautiful coastal scenery accessible to walkers, sightseers, and maybe more than a few transport enthusiasts too.